THE FLAG HERITAGE FOUNDATION MONOGRAPH AND TRANSLATION SERIES

PUBLICATION No. 4

THE DOUBLE EAGLE

BY DAVID F. PHILLIPS

FLAG
HERITAGE
FOUNDATION

2014

THE FLAG HERITAGE FOUNDATION
MONOGRAPH AND TRANSLATION SERIES

The Flag Heritage Foundation was established in 1971 in order, among other purposes, "to collect, organize, and disseminate information concerning all aspects of flags and related symbols" and "to promote wide public knowledge of the rich history of flags which fosters international understanding and respect for national heritage." It is a registered charity in the Commonwealth of Massachusetts.

T e Flag Heritage Foundation Monograph and Translation Series was established in 2009 to publish worthy monographs on flags and related subjects, and to translate and publish in English works previously appearing only in languages inaccessible to most scholars. This is the fourth publication in this series.

Price: US $20 (plus shipping)

Non-profit organizations, libraries, and vexillological and heraldic organizations
may obtain copies *gratis* or at a reduced rate – inquire of the Foundation.

PREVIOUSLY PUBLISHED

THE ESTONIAN FLAG, by Prof. Dr. Karl Aun………….. 2009
EMBLEMS OF THE INDIAN STATES, by David F. Phillips…….2011
HISTORY OF THE FLAG OF HAITIAN INDEPENDENCE, by Odette Roy Fombrun…..2013

TABLE OF CONTENTS

This book is dedicated
with respect and affection to

Dr. Whitney Smith

pioneering scholar and beloved friend

PREFACE

An eagle with two heads – the first question is what to call it. Although similar forms appear in many distant and often unrelated cultures, *our* eagle – meaning the two-headed eagle we know from Germany and Austria and Russia, and elsewhere in Europe, traces back to the medieval Near East. In Greek it is *dikephalos* – the two-headed one – a word hardly known in the West. There is no really suitable single word available in English, but as usual the Germans have a compact and exact term. They call it *der Doppeladler* – the *double eagle*, and as the English alternatives are all awkward and ungainly, that is the name I will use for it in this book.[1]

I first noticed the double eagle as a child, when I was given a copy of *Flags of Maritime Nations*, the United States Navy's official flag book.[2] This magnificent volume illustrated the flags of the nations, in beautiful color lithographs, so our warships could recognize them and render the appropriate courtesies and salutes. For this reason it included not just the main national flags, but for important countries the flags of kings and high officials, naval officers and government departments.[3]

In 1899 Austria and Russia were still functioning empires, and their emperors had grand and complicated imperial standards, which were illustrated in the book. The Russian imperial standard on land was a black double eagle on a golden field, and the eagle had such a wealth of intricate elements – crowns, ribbons, a scepter and orb, and nine shields – that it was illustrated separately, larger so the details could be understood. That very eagle is reproduced in color on the inside back cover of this book.

I won't say that eagle got me started on heraldry, the inexhaustible study that I have been learning from for the last 65 years, but it helped. The eagle had so many embellishments

---

[1]   It is unfortunate that in the United States a $10 gold piece was known as an *eagle*, and so a $20 gold piece was a *double eagle*. If you Google *double eagle* this coin, and things named for it, account for most of the first results. Neither coin has been minted since 1933.

[2]   Washington, 5th ed. 1899.

[3]   A few countries with the largest navies – Britain, France, Germany, Russia, the United States – issued these books from roughly the mid-19th to the mid-20th century. They are obsolete now, although still beautiful – the French *Pavilions Nationaux et Marques Distinctives* (Paris, 2000) was the last of the comprehensive volumes.

– the shields on its wings, with their distinctive views seen as through windows, the elaborate golden chain and the crucified saint, and the scepter with the fascinating infinite regression – a miniature of the eagle held another scepter, which presumably (although too small to see) had *another* miniature holding *another* scepter, *ad infinitum*. Also the eagle had *style* – its piercing eyes, its fierce beak and tongue, its shaggy thighs, the subtle curvings of a tail certainly unknown in nature, the delicate secondary feathers – on close examination not really feathers but just undulating lines – between the main pinions of the wings. There was a lot to learn about that eagle.

And it had two heads! The same book showed another two-headed eagle (for Austria) and yet another (very small, for Serbia) – they were not the same, or were they? I had a lot to learn here too, just how much I did not realize until decades later.

This book is an exploration of the double eagle image, but it is not a definitive treatise. It touches on the history and culture of many nations over almost a thousand years, but I have by no means mastered any of these, and cannot even read some of the languages. I have been guided by the images I found in my research, but for every image I used, I left out many, many more. If I had chosen different images, my story would have been different in detail (although not I hope in general outline), and some of my conclusions might have been different too. I raise many questions I have not answered, and suggest some areas where more research is needed.

That an essay on so particular and restricted a subject could have reached this length – and it could have been much longer – shows how heraldry, and by extension all culture, is truly a seamless web. For everything leads to something else; nothing makes sense without context, including the context itself. A carving in a church in Bolivia (Figure 213) leads us back centuries to a ceramic tile in a palace in Asia Minor (Figure 8), and then forward again to the logo of a Greek football team playing perhaps this week (Figure 229). Our understanding of nothing is ever really complete – there is always more to learn. Perhaps the most remarkable thing about this particular web of cultural connections is that at its center is something that never existed – there is no such thing as a two-headed eagle, really, only the *idea* of one. But the history of the world – half the world, anyway – of empires and wars and exploration and trade and money and politics and art – can be reached through that idea.

I have many people to thank for help in bringing this work to completion.

- Annie Platoff and Amy Segal for help with Russian, Gerald Stiebel and Hanns Hohmann for help with German, Christopher Phillips for help with French, Khalid Obeid for help with Arabic, Brother William Short, O.F.M., for help with Latin, and Tatiana Tsakiropoulou-Summers and Ioannis Stamos for help with Greek.

- Scot Guenter, Christina Lazaridi, and Roland Moore for help in finding people, Jörg Karaschewski and Andreas Herzfeld for help with German flags, Dr. Peter Diem for help with an Austrian emblem, Željko Heimer for help with Montenegro (and especially for helping me guard against errors in the Balkan section – all that remain are my fault), Noah Phillips for help with a line drawing (Figure 39), Charles Waltmire for redrawing the map and several illustrations, Klaudia Nelson for the photograph on page 159, and Robert Rosoff for his careful proofreading of the text.

- Columbia University librarians Mary Lynn Cargill at the Butler Library reference desk and Zak Rouse and Kitty Chibnik at the Avery Architecture and Fine Arts Library, Zoe Stansell at the British Library Manuscripts Reference Service, Dennis J. Sears at the University of Illinois Rare Book & Manuscript Library, Linda Karr O'Connor at the Hugh & Hazel Darling Law Library of the University of California, Los Angeles, Scott Tiffney at the American Philatelic Society Research Library, Katie Rissetto and Elizabeth Hahn Benge at the American Numismatic Society Library, Ann Dorman and Jenny Rockwell at the San Francisco Public Library (and also the librarians of the SFPL Inter-Library Loan Service, to whom I owe a special debt), and the librarians at the Thomas J. Watson Art History Library at the Metropolitan Museum of Art in New York.

- Internet writers, sometimes anonymous, and especially Hubert de Vries, Dr. Peter Diem, Jaume Ollé and Željko Heimer.

- Eugenio Ajroldi di Robbiate at the Sovereign Order of Malta, Ralf Hartemink at Heraldry of the World, Johann Hanslmeier at the Austrian Mint, Peter Orensky at TMEALF, Kathy Forer at Foreverink, Alex Best at Simple Solutions, Wordmaster Will James for formatting help, Maria Lappa at the Deltion of the Christian Archaeological Society of Greece, and Arianna Louise Phillips for her patience and clear judgment.

- My grandmother, Ida J. Rubinstein (1890-1962), who got me started in this study as a child by giving me my first serious heraldic books, including one that was the source of several illustrations in this book.

- The Board of Trustees of the Flag Heritage Foundation, all distinguished scholars, for their understanding and unstinting support of my work, without whom this book would never have been written, and Debbie Waltmire of Specialty Graphics, without whom it might never have been printed.

- And finally, **SRI LORD GANESHA**, the great god of India, Ageless Large-Eared Lord, Mighty and Auspicious, Elephant-Headed Patron of Learning and Literature, Inspiration and Scribe.

While I am thanking people, I feel I must say that in writing this history I have made use of the works of many great scholars, now dead – men like Gustav Seyler, Otto Posse, Hugo Gerard Ströhl, Otto Hupp, Maximilian Gritzner, Heinrich Philipp Cappe, Émile Gevaert, Alexander Soloviev, Ignacio Vicente Cascante and Edward Twining, to name only a few. Many of them were also outstanding heraldic artists. Their work is acknowledged in the footnotes and in the Sources of the Illustrations, and again here as representative of the timeless and boundless community of scholarship. Without the intense and prolonged labor of these scholars and hundreds of others, I would know nothing. A respect for their achievements obliges me to admit, to myself and to my readers, that this book is the offering of a dilettante. If successful, it will have illuminated the surface of its subject, but not its depths.

San Francisco
September, 2014

AUTHOR'S NOTE

I relied for a large part of the research for this book on my own heraldic reference library, augmented by material in other libraries. But I also relied to a great extent on Internet resources.

The Internet is very new, and the amazing wealth of information it makes so easily available requires revising some scholarly prejudices. Scholars trained in the old ways of research have a skeptical attitude toward the Internet. Skepticism is appropriate, but snobbery isn't. Yes, not everything on the Internet is necessarily true, but not everything in print is necessarily true either.

It would have been very difficult to research this material without Internet resources, especially the Google search engine and extra-especially Google Images, Wikipedia, access to Google and Wikipedia in other languages, Google Translate, and Wikimedia Commons. I tried to exercise reasonable scholarly judgment in assessing information from the Internet, by triangulating research using more than one source, and by focusing research on images. Thus for example, when investigating a specific *fact* (for example, who ruled a particular principality on a specific date), I was content to *begin* with Wikipedia, but I sought confirmation from other sources, both electronic and print. And facts are different from conclusions – I was willing to accept *facts* from the Internet, suitably confirmed, but I formed my own *conclusions* from the facts.

Focusing on images was a powerful technique for avoiding error. Thus I would not claim, based on some author's bare assertion, that the double eagle was used as a symbol of power in 17th century Romania. But if I could coax from the Internet the image of a coin, that was different – there it was, in hard metal, with an inscription and maybe a date, and the image of the eagle.[1] You can usually trust a coin or a seal or a monument where mere words might not be enough. I could also work backwards – having first found an image of a coin, for example through Google Images, I had a core around which to build context and an anchor against which to test assertions, both those of others and my own.

Google Images provided access to a vast treasury of visual data from many sources, not all of them scholarly. For example, a coin might first be encountered on the eBay Internet auction site, or in a Wikimedia gallery, or on someone's anonymous blog, and then could

---

[1]   See Figure 194; and on this technique see my article "Coins as a Heraldic Resource" at tinyurl.com/mwv8qhq.

be verified and described and perhaps dated in the numismatic literature. Often this literature was available in digital form, through the Google Books Library Project or otherwise. Access to Wikipedia and Google in other languages broadened my reach enormously. Google Translate helped me with languages I could *sort* of read, and gave me access to material – not only articles but context for images – in languages I could not read even a little. I would have had almost no access to what I needed to understand the development of the double eagle image in, for example, Serbia, without Google Translate.

Another valuable use of the Internet has been to let me direct my readers to resources, visual and textual, more easily accessible than rare and obscure books only found in great libraries. I have been very liberal with footnotes partly to point out these resources to readers in a way that was not possible before the Internet. With rare exceptions I have converted Internet addresses to tinyurl format. These tinyurl addresses, with their unique seven-character codes, provide *nearly permanent* links to web pages anywhere on the Internet.[2] They are preferable to original web addresses because the originals (especially for specific pages, and those presented in non-Latin scripts) can go on for hundreds of characters of code and be almost impossible to copy accurately from a printed book. I have underlined tinyurls (and the occasional unmediated web address) for easy identification. Tinyurls will of course not work after a website goes dead and can be traced only through the Internet Archive or some similar repository of expired material. But I have been careful to identify web pages by name where possible, to help in this circumstance. Internet articles in foreign languages may be roughly translated by copying the url into Google Translate.

Two other Internet resources were especially useful. Flags of the World, at www.crwflags.com/fotw/flags, hosts a rich accumulation of information about flags and state symbols of many kinds, and well-constructed images. Although the postings on this site are only individual opinions, I have found FOTW a very valuable *starting place* for many purposes, where supplementary and dissenting views are responsibly noted and developed. And it would have been very difficult to check, correct, and where necessary complete citations without Worldcat, www.worldcat.org, a bibliographic reference tool and unified library catalogue of nearly incalculable power.

I have been liberal with footnotes, not only for citations and image references but where I felt additional information would be useful, but might be distracting in the main text. I may have been *so* liberal with footnotes that they are distracting anyway. Although I feel these sidelights illuminate the story usefully, some may find it easier to follow the main argument by ignoring the footnotes altogether.

---

[2]   See www.tinyurl.com. *Url* means *uniform resource locator*, commonly known as a web address.

I have translated foreign words wherever they appear, even titles of books and names of institutions. Why not? But for clarity and simplicity, I have deliberately put these translations almost entirely into lower case letters, even where this varies from customary English usage. Where I have translated passages of *text* from a foreign language myself, I have indicated this with the notation (tr. DFP). I have generally but not always followed local capitalization norms in citing works in foreign languages. Transliteration of words from languages normally written in non-Latin scripts – mainly Cyrillic, but also Greek – may be a bit idiosyncratic. With an occasional considered exception I have standardized the spelling of the name *Palaeologue*, unless in a direct quotation. I have westernized Greek and Balkan given names, such as Theodore and Andronicus, that have easy equivalents – *Theodoros* would be pedantic. The word *colour*, spelled in the British way, has the specific meaning of a regimental or unit flag. It have capitalized the word *empire* where it clearly refers to a particular empire that would have been capitalized if fully named.

I have tried to avoid abbreviations, but I do sometimes use c. for *circa* [about] in a date, vol., fig., n., no. and p[p]. for volume, figure, note, number and page[s] in a citation, and *id.* and *ibid.* for immediate duplication of citations. As is customary, n.d. and n.p. in citations mean *no date* and *no place* of publication is given.

The section headed *Sources of the Illustrations* collects the sources of *all* the illustrations, including the covers, text figures, gallery, and ornamental figures. Most of the images are in the public domain, or are reproduced under a general license (for example from Wikimedia Commons and Flags of the World) governed by special permission protocols. But even where not, their reproduction here constitutes fair use under the copyright statute (17 U.S.C. § 107), which provides in pertinent part that

> [i]n determining whether the use made of a work in any particular case is a fair use the factors to be considered shall include (1) the purpose and character of the use, including whether such use is of a commercial nature or is for nonprofit educational purposes; (2) the nature of the copyrighted work; (3) the amount and substantiality of the portion used in relation to the copyrighted work as a whole; and (4) the effect of the use upon the potential market for or value of the copyrighted work.

This is a scholarly work published by a non-profit foundation, not commercially or for profit. With rare exceptions, I have taken only a very small insubstantial portion – one or maybe two images – from any single source. These uses – always explicitly acknowledged where acknowledgment is possible, have no effect on the potential market for or value of any copyrighted work.[3] Moreover, where the image is a photograph of a

---

[3] A few images have been taken from blogs where they were posted without attribution, or have become untraceable where an Internet source can no longer be found.

work of art or history that is itself out of copyright, there is no copyright in the reproducing image. *Bridgeman Art Library v. Corel Corp.*, 36 F. Supp. 2d 191 (S.D.N.Y. 1999). Please write to me at <u>dfp18@columbia.edu</u> if you feel I have made unfair use of your published work.

MAP

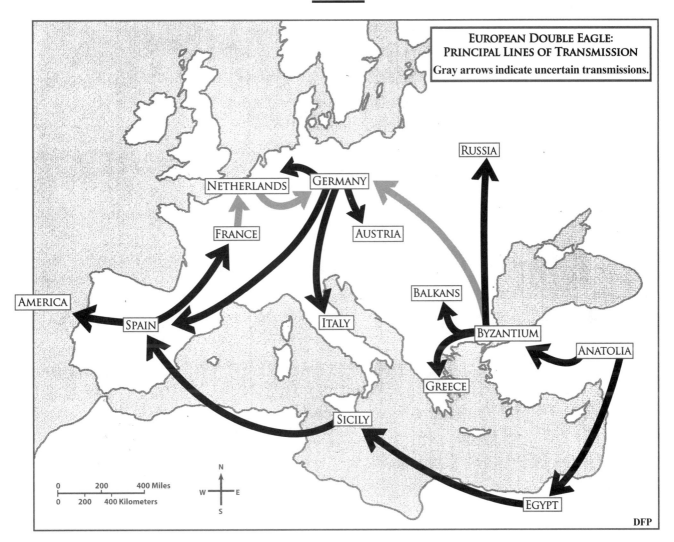

DIFFUSION OF THE DOUBLE EAGLE IMAGE IN EUROPE

COLLEGIUM POETARUM. WOODCUT BY HANS BURGKMAIR THE ELDER (1510).

14

THE DOUBLE EAGLE

by David F. Phillips

**Numbered figures appear in the Gallery of Illustrations, beginning on page 91.
Notes on the sources of *all* the illustrations begin on page 139.**

The eagle with two heads appears as a folk or religious image in many cultures, but the eagle of this book is the European heraldic double eagle that was the emblem of the German, Austrian and Russian empires. This book follows the double eagle's history as a highly influential image in the revived Western (or Holy Roman) Empire, and elsewhere in many other countries of Europe, and later long after the end of both empires and in some places even today.[1]

THE NEAR EASTERN BACKGROUND

The image of the double eagle is not indigenous to Western Europe, and was scarcely known there before the 12th century. And where it was known, it was imported from the East (counting Islamic Spain as an outpost of the East).

The earliest known double eagle appears on a cylinder seal from the Sumerian city of Lagash around 2500 BC (Figure 1). It was also displayed by the Hittites, relics of whose civilization in Anatolia (now Asian Turkey) include the great double eagle carved into the stone of Alaca Höyük (Eyük) (Figure 2) and a cylinder seal impression from Boğazkale [Bogazköy] (Figure 3). But there is no reason to think that there is any Sumerian or Hittite connection to our eagle.[2]

The Hittite Empire fell around 1180 BC, and while there are occasional examples of the double eagle in the Near East in the intervening centuries, it does not reappear more than occasionally for about 2200 years. Around the 12th century AD there was an efflorescence of this image within the Great Seljuk Empire in what is now eastern Turkey and Mesopotamia. The Seljuks were Moslem in religion and Turko-Persian in culture, as was

---

[1] The image above is of an imperial herald of the 16th century.

[2] Double-eagle ornaments were also found by Schliemann in Bronze Age Mycenae – see Figure 4.

their Anatolian successor the Sultanate of Rum, centered in Konya, Turkey (the former Iconium).[3] Amida (modern Diyarbakır, Turkey), once Seljuk and later subject to the (Turkmen) Artuquid dynasty, was another important center for this image. Figures 5-7 are examples from Amida; Figures 8-10 are from Konya.[4] Both these places are in roughly the same region of eastern Anatolia as the Hittite relics. Figure 11 is a Zengid coin, from an area somewhat to the east of Konya. We have *no evidence* of any direct link between the Hittites and the Seljuk Turks. But it seems *intuitively* more likely that the double eagle continued in the undocumented folklore of the local population than that such a bizarre creature was independently re-imagined in the same location.[5]

The motif of the double eagle, along with other elements of Turko-Persian culture, spread along well-established trade and cultural highways to Moslem communities further west.[6] Thus it appeared in Egypt – Figures 12-15 show four examples.[7] It was well known in Sicily, a mixing bowl of Latin, Greek and Islamic cultures. Figure 16 is a textile preserved in Palermo.[8] Figure 17 is an 11th century wall decoration from the cathedral in

---

[3]   *Anatolia*, now meaning roughly all of Asian Turkey, was the name of a Byzantine *theme* or military-administrative district – the word comes from the Greek *anatolē* [ανατολή], meaning roughly *sunrise*, a poetic way of saying *east of Constantinople*. The name *Rum* was derived from *Rome*; the Turks established this sultanate in territory formerly Roman (as the Byzantines called their country).

[4]   In the Turko-Persian cultural sphere Islam permitted images of animals, forbidding depiction only of the human form. On the basis of carvings such as that in Figure 9, the double eagle has been described as the emblem, and even as the *coat of arms*, of the Great Seljuk Empire. Perhaps so, but I am unaware of any *actual evidence* of this.

[5]   There are scattered references in the literature suggesting an origin for this image deeper into Central Asia. Fortunately it is not necessary to decide that question here, or the possible identification of the Near Eastern double eagle with the fearsome giant *hamca* (*haga*, *anqa*) bird of Turkish and Arabic legend.

[6]   I am grateful to the distinguished Serbian historian Alexander Soloviev (1890-1971), whose essay "Les Emblèmes héraldiques de Byzance et des Slaves" [Heraldic emblems of Byzantium and of the Slavs], Seminarium Kondakovianum (Prague, 1935), 7:119-164, is a masterful summary of the scholarship on this subject and has formed a framework for my own understanding of it. Although old, it is the most comprehensive treatment of the topic I have found and is still respectfully cited. I am also grateful to the Dutch heraldic scholar Hubert de Vries, whose learned and generously illustrated Hubert-Herald articles helped focus my understanding of many aspects of the double eagle's career in East and West. Tinyurl.com/kqezyhk links to his article "Two-Headed Eagle," with many illustrations, some in color.

[7]   The incense burner in Figure 12 is discussed in Leo A. Mayer, *Saracenic Heraldry* (Oxford, 1933), 112.

[8]   See Soloviev (1935), note 6, 128. It is recorded in a Sicilian inventory as early as 1309. The inscription on its wings, though in Arabic script, does not appear actually to be Arabic, which suggests local non-Islamic manufacture.

Palermo; similar decorations are found in other Norman buildings there.[9] A series of coins, issued at Messina for Frederick II as King of Sicily during his minority in 1202-03, also bear a double eagle, along with a pseudo-Kufic inscription and a Greek reverse.[10] See Figure 18.

Most important of all was Spain, most of which was Moslem from the eighth century. Cordoba especially was a great *entrepôt* where Christian, Moslem and Jewish cultures mixed relatively freely, and was one of the main entry points of Islamic art into Western Europe. Many examples of double-eagle textiles from Islamic Spain still survive; they were sometimes used as gravecloths in Christian shrines. Figures 19-22 are examples from Spain, France, Germany and Switzerland. There were once hundreds more, and local craftsmen probably made others on similar patterns. From Spain the double eagle image spread north as a motif in the Romanesque churches and manuscript illuminations of 12th century France.[11] Figures 23-28 are examples.[12]

BYZANTIUM

The Roman Empire included all the territories bordering the Mediterranean Sea and many more besides. In 285 AD the Emperor Diocletian divided the empire for administrative purposes into two sections, East and West. In 330 Constantine the Great moved the capital of the empire to Byzantium (present-day Istanbul), which he renamed Constantinople after himself. In 476 the Western Empire fell to the Germanic warlord Odoacer, and was soon extinguished, but the Roman Empire continued in the East – this is what we now call the Byzantine Empire, although as noted it called itself simply *Rome*.[13]

---

9   See Pascal Androudis, "Les premières apparitions attestées de l'aigle bicéphale dans l'art roman d'Occident (XIe-XIIe siècles): Origines et symbolique" [The first appearances of the two-headed eagle in the Romanesque art of the West (11th-12th centuries): Origins and symbolism], *Nis and Byzantium* (Niš, Serbia, 2013), 11:210-225, at 213-17.

10   Kufic is a style of Arabic script; *pseudo-Kufic* writing is an approximate copy of it by artisans not actually literate in the script. It was found often in Western works in many media, for example in paintings trying to depict Near Eastern textiles. Rodolfo Spahr's standard catalogue, *Monete Siciliane dai Bizantini a Carlo I d'Angiò (582-1282)* [Sicilian coins from the Byzantines to Charles I of Anjou, 582-1282] (Zürich 1976), 186, calls this issue (No. 45) pseudo-Kufic, while Alberto Varesi, *Monete Italiane Regionali* [Italian regional coins] (Pavia, 2011), 29, calls it (No. 73) "Kufic, indecipherable." I am going with pseudo-Kufic.

11   See Androudis (2013), note 9, 217-223, where this idea is developed in detail.

12   See the map on page 13, illustrating the diffusion of the double eagle image in Europe.

13   "The Byzantine Empire was the continuation in Christian form of the ancient Roman Empire." Donald M. Nicol, *The End of the Byzantine Empire* (London, 1979), 6.

The *single*-headed eagle had of course been an important emblem of Rome since ancient times. It was identified with Jupiter, king of the Roman gods, and with the Roman state and army, and later with the divinity of the emperors. The single-headed eagle continued to be identified with the Roman Empire until its very end. But there was no trace of a *double* eagle in Rome, west or east, until it entered the vocabulary of Byzantine ornament through the Near Eastern sources mentioned above.[14] It was not, at the start, any more important or specific than many other animal forms, such as lions, camels, gazelles and peacocks.[15]

In its standard stereotyped form the Near Eastern double eagle was pleasingly symmetrical (very suitable for a tessellated pattern), had two heads but only one neck, and usually held a beast of prey in each talon. Its symmetry may be the key to its popularity as an emblem – this was available to artists because an eagle could be presented frontally, wings and legs spread evenly (*spread-eagle*, or in heraldic terms *displayed*), with only the head on one side or the other. A second head completed the symmetry, something not possible for any other archetypal animal. Indeed, as one writer put it:

> In the late Byzantine period, the motif of the two-headed eagle took precedence over the rest because it was regarded as ideal, according to the prevailing aesthetic criteria. Losing its mimetic character, it became a motif drawn in a single line, and its symmetry became the dominant feature. Its coloring was no longer realistic but acquired an emblematic character.[16]

"What do we know about the double eagle at Byzantium?" asked the historian Alexander Soloviev, who answered "in truth, little enough."[17] Our actual knowledge of the Byzantine double eagle is uncomfortably slight, beyond generalizations from a few surviving images, mostly architectural details and representations of patterns on court clothing and on the special cushions (called *suppedia*) on which imperial figures were shown standing. The vast record of coins and seals that helps us understand the development of the double eagle in the West is not much help with Byzantine practice.[18] But Byzantium is often

---

[14]   See, e.g., Anna Muthesius, "The Byzantine Eagle," in her *Studies in Silk in Byzantium* (London, 2004), 228.

[15]   Cf., e.g., Bojan Popović, "Imperial Usage of Zoömorphic Motifs on Textiles: the Two-Headed Eagle and the Lion in Circles and Between Crosses in the Late Byzantine Period," IKON (Rijeka [Croatia], 2009), 2:127-136.

[16]   *Id.*, 133.

[17]   "*À vrai dire, assez peu.*" Soloviev (1935), note 6, 129.

[18]   "The emblem of the two-headed eagle plays virtually no role on Palaeologan coins." Philip Grierson and Alfred R. Bellinger, Catalogue of the Byzantine Coins in the Dumbarton Oaks

(footnote continues →)

mentioned as the source of the Western double eagle, and because this assumption does not seem justified it seems useful to discuss its actual use there in some detail.

The time of the double eagle's first appearance at the Byzantine court "lies yet in darkness."[19] Soloviev says:

> it is quite difficult to pinpoint the first appearance of the double eagle in Byzantium. It is certain that this appearance cannot be given a precise date, and it was not due to any act of a sovereign introducing a new emblem. To the contrary, its use grew imperceptibly. Under the influence of the Eastern style so powerful in Byzantium, the double eagle first appeared as ornament, on brocades and bas-reliefs. As neither use survives except in undated fragments, the earliest data can be only approximations.[20]

From painted images on documents and frescoes we can see eagles (both single and double) on the silks and brocades and embroideries used for the robes of imperial dynasts with the court titles *sebastocrator*, *despot* and *caesar*. The eagles seem to have been part of the system of rank insignia, similar in some ways to that used by the mandarins of China under the Ch'ing Dynasty (1644-1912), with their phoenixes and cranes.[21]

The surviving representations of Byzantine double-eagle robes are now mostly damaged and faded. The examples I have seen look remarkably alike, the distinctions among them evident only to specialists in Byzantine costume. Even the best do not reproduce well in black and white.[22] Accordingly I have reproduced only one, Figure 30, that must stand

---

(*footnote continues ...*)

      Collection ..." (Washington, 1999), 5:85. The Palaeologues were the last Byzantine dynasty; their rule dates from 1261.

[19]   "*... liegt immer in Dunkeln.*" Charalampos Chotzakoglou, "Die Palaiologen und das früheste Auftreten des byzantinischen Doppeladlers" [The Palaeologues and the first appearance of the Byzantine double eagle], *Byzantinoslavica* (Prague, 1996), 57:60.

[20]   Soloviev (1935), note 6, 130 (tr. DFP).

[21]   See, e.g., C. A. S. Williams, *Outlines of Chinese Symbolism and Art Motives* (Shanghai, 3d revised ed. 1941; modern reprint New York, 1975), 87-92. For lovely examples of the square silk rank badges of Chinese mandarins, see the Pinterest posting "Chinese Mandarin Squares" at tinyurl.com/pwfbj84.

[22]   The Byzantines had garment patterns in striking black and white rectangles that reproduce quite well, but the eagles (often within circular frames) were usually in muted red and gold.

for the others. It shows the sebastocrator Constantine Palaeologue, wearing a double-eagle robe, in his mid-14th century donor portrait in the Lincoln Typikon.[23]

Despot (Greek *despotēs*, δεσπότης) was a title given to imperial princes and other senior members of the imperial family. The word means roughly *lord*, like the Latin *dominus*. Although despots were sometimes given subsidiary territories to rule, subject to imperial oversight, the term did not necessarily imply specific authority, or have the absolutist connotation of the modern English word *despot*. The title was also used in the Greek-ruled territories during the period of Western domination in Constantinople (the Latin Empire, 1204-61), and later by some Christian rulers there and in the Balkans. *Sebastocrator* and *caesar* were likewise titles reserved for senior imperial princes – they were personal titles, not implying territorial jurisdiction as western titles often did.

On occasion a despot or consort (but significantly, not the emperor himself) appears in a robe decorated with double eagles. Indeed, the emperor is often shown in robes without a double-eagle pattern, while other members of his family have one. A telling example is a notable miniature in a book called the *Corpus Dionysiacum*, given by the ambassador of Emperor Manuel II to the Abbey of St. Denis in 1408 and now in the Louvre.[24] The emperor and empress appear with three of their sons. The two younger ones – both of whom, Theodore and Andronicus, had the title *despotēs* – wore robes decorated with double-eagle medallions, but the imperial couple did not. This alone seems sufficient evidence that even in the early 15th century the double eagle was not a mark of the imperial office.

High-end patterned Byzantine silk textiles are sometimes suggested as the medium for transmitting the double eagle into the West. Such silks were given by the imperial government as official gifts, and were then passed on within Western lands by magnates and churchmen and used as vestments, to adorn the tombs of saints, and for other

---

[23] A monastic typikon is a foundation charter, setting out the rule and procedures for an Orthodox monastery. Unlike the practice in the West, where monasteries usually followed the rule of a religious order, Orthodox monasteries were often individual aristocratic foundations with idiosyncratic rules. The Lincoln Typikon is in the Bodleian Library in Oxford – see Wikimedia Commons at tinyurl.com/n8cm5az for a color image. For more about it see, e.g., Cecily Hennessy, "The Lincoln College Typikon: Influences of Church and Family in an Illuminated Foundation Document for a Palaiologan Convent in Constantinople," in John Lowden and Alixe Bovey, eds., *Under the Influence: The Concept of Influence and the Study of Illuminated Manuscripts* (Turnhout [Belgium], 2007).

[24] It was an edition of the works of the sixth century Christian writer known as Pseudo-Dionysius the Areopagite. The miniature may be seen on the University of Oklahoma's website at tinyurl.com/mv22ad2. The image and its historical and iconographic context are exhaustively discussed in Cecily J. Hilsdale, *Byzantine Art and Diplomacy in an Age of Decline* (Cambridge, 2014), 236-63 and plate 8.

purposes.[25] But this seems an unlikely source for the Western double eagle. Many of the eagle textiles that used to be considered Byzantine turn out on a more sophisticated analysis to be Islamic Spanish. The few surviving genuine Byzantine eagle silks in the West show *single*-headed eagles. Examples include the Shroud of St. Germanus (see the line drawing in Figure 29), and the *Adlerkasel* [eagle cope] in the Diocesan Museum of Brixen in the Italian Tyrol (whose eagles look very similar and may have come from the same workshop).[26] No double-eagle silk of undoubted Byzantine origin still survives, in East or West.[27]

While the double eagle did have a role in imperial iconography, it was not the *imperial arms* in the Western heraldic sense of being the official emblem of the state, as it became in the German and later empires. Instead it had what has been aptly called a "long-standing but broad imperial significance."[28] It was an "element of imperial pomp"[29] without actually being a specific designator either of the emperor or of the state.[30] As Babuin says, "there is no iconographical evidence of the use of the two-headed eagle as the official device of the Byzantine State."[31]

---

[25] Silk was a Byzantine state monopoly – the method of its manufacture, smuggled out of China long before, was a closely guarded secret. For more on Byzantium's use of silks as diplomatic gifts, see Anna Muthesius, "Silk, Power and Diplomacy in Byzantium," *Textile Society of America Proceedings* (Berkeley [California], 1992), 3:99-110, at 101-3.

[26] The Shroud of St. Germanus is in the Museum of the Abbey of St.-Germain in Auxerre, France. The original from which the line drawing in Figure 29 was made may be seen on the museum's website at tinyurl.com/lkapje7, and a better image on a French blogspot at tinyurl.com/odgrfr8. The *Adlerkasel* may be seen on the Brixen Museum's website at tinyurl.com/qzz8uzs.

[27] Muthesius (2004), note 14, 28. There are a few non-Spanish double eagle textiles – the Shroud (or Carpet) of St. Knud in Odense, Denmark, the eagle silk of Siegburg, and a silk (now lost) from Quedlinburg, both in Germany – but they are all now thought to have been made elsewhere. The Carpet of St. Knud may be seen on the Danish History website at tinyurl.com/m6wunk5, the Quedlinburg silk may be seen in Muthesius (2004), plate 61, and the Siegburg eagle silk in Anna Muthesius, *Byzantine Silk Weaving AD 400 to AD 1200* (Vienna, 1997), plate 91A. The 1997 work, a *magnum opus* and grand catalogue of Byzantine silks, discusses these three pieces at 47-50.

[28] The phrase was used by Joseph D. Alchermes in his essay "The Bulgarians," in Helen C. Evans and William D. Wixom, *The Glory of Byzantium: Art and Culture of the Middle Byzantine Era AD 843-1261* (New York, 1997), 327, discussing a double eagle on a 10th-11th century stone slab from Zagora in Bulgaria (shown as a text figure on page 159 below).

[29] "*Un élément du faste impérial.*" Soloviev (1935), note 6, 137.

[30] Chotzakoglou, note 19, 66, calls it a "symbol of the power of the empire" [*Herrschaftssymbol des Kaisertums*].

[31] Andrea Babuin, "Standards and Insignia of Byzantium," *Byzantion* (Brussels, 2001), 71(1):5-59, 38.

Neither was it the *coat of arms of the imperial family* in a heraldic sense, at least until near the end of the Empire.

> We must consider that family coats of arms are not known for Byzantine noble houses. Neither on inscriptions or seals, or in other pictorial representations, do we find Byzantine family arms [*Familienwappen*] in the Western sense. There are only family monograms. On this view there is no reason for the House of Palaeologue to adopt family arms. The argument from Western influence suggests the question why the imperial example found no other imitator among the Byzantine nobility.[32]

In 1204 the Fourth Crusade, coming mostly from France and the Low Countries, overwhelmed the already much-reduced Byzantine Empire, replaced it with a Latin Empire, and partitioned Greece and parts of the Balkans and Greek Islands into Latin-ruled states (and some successor Greek states).[33] See the image below.[34]

---

[32]   Chotzakoglou, note 19, 66 (tr. DFP).

[33]   This episode is unusually well-documented because the French historian Geoffroi de Ville-hardouin (1160 - c. 1212) was present and recorded his recollections in the classic history *De la Conquête de Constantinople* [On the conquest of Constantinople]. An English translation (by Frank T. Marzels (London, 1908) is available digitally on Fordham University's website at tinyurl.com/n433vf5. A good modern account is Jonathan Phillips, *The Fourth Crusade and the Sack of Constantinople* (New York, 2004).

[34]   The image of the Crusader attack on Constantinople is taken from an edition of Villehardouin's history (see note 33) published in manuscript in Venice around 1330. The flag above the city is the tetragrammatic cross ensign discussed at pages 23-24 below, and see Babuin (note 31) – unusually, the Bs are placed horizontally. Note that the army on the right carries a flag with the lion arms of Baldwin of Flanders, who established the Latin Empire in Constantinople after his victory. The shield borne by the same army bears the arms of Brabant, but the Duke of Brabant did not take part in this crusade.

Western heraldic forms did make an impression in the Byzantine world during the period of the Latin Empire, whose magnates and officials used heraldic seals in the usual Western fashion.[35] And after the restoration of the Empire in 1261 there were some examples of the double eagle used in the Western heraldic manner. For example, Soloviev mentions a seal of Theodore Palaeologue, Despot of Morea in Greece, attached to a document dated 1391, showing him in proper heraldic style with a shield (unfortunately now effaced) and a helmet with a double-eagle crest.[36] And Princess Tamar Comnena had a gold and enamel locket alternating the double eagle with her husband's arms of Anjou (Figure 31).[37]

But generally, it may be a mistake even to look for a Byzantine analogue to Western heraldic display. "As a matter of fact," writes Andrea Babuin, "Orthodox Christian Europe prove[d] not to share the vivid interest in heraldry that spread in the west from the

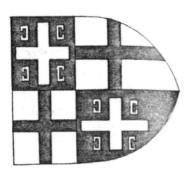

beginning of the 11th century ..."[38] The Empire's coins and seals usually made use of religious imagery rather than personal emblems, as did Western coins before heraldry.

The *tetragrammatic cross* (a cross *cantoning* the letter B in each corner) was closer to a state

---

[35] But not with the double eagle – the Latin emperors used arms of quite a different pattern: on red, a gold cross with five smaller gold crosses in each quarter, the central one within a golden ring. This design was clearly based on Byzantine textiles. See the equestrian seal in Gustav Schlumberger, *Un Nouveau Sceau de L'Empire Latin* [A new seal of the Latin Empire] (Paris 1901), 4 (reprinted from *Révue Numismatique* [Numismatic review] (Paris, 1901), 396 ff.), showing Latin Emperor Henri I with these arms. A similar seal, with other helpful illustrations of the arms of the Latin emperors, can be seen in Hubert de Vries' article "Byzantium: Arms and Emblems" at <u>tinyurl.com/l3fw353</u>.

[36] Soloviev (1935), note 6, 134; see also Dan Cervodeanu, "Contributions à l'étude de l'héraldique byzantine et postbyzantine" [Contributions to the study of Byzantine and post-Byzantine heraldry], *Jahrbuch der Oesterreichischen Byzantinistik* [Yearbook of Austrian Byzantine studies] (Vienna, 1982), 32(2):409-22, at 414-15.

[37] This beautiful object, dated to 1294 and fashioned in the shape of an ivy leaf, is preserved in the Museo Archeologico Nazionale [National archaeological museum] of Cividale dei Friuli in Italy. For more on Princess Tamar, see Donald M. Nicol, *The Byzantine Lady* (Cambridge, 1996), 24-32 and plate 8. Her Angevin husband was Philip of Taranto.

[38] Babuin, note 31, 7-8. The beginning of the 11th century seems more than 100 years too early.

symbol than the double eagle.[39] The B's were traditionally understood to stand for the motto *Basileus basileōn, basileuōn basileuontōn* [King of kings, ruling over kings], and while this exact translation has fallen out of favor, it probably had a similar meaning.[40] This device, rather than the eagle, was used on Byzantine battle flags.[41] The anonymous Franciscan who set out what he thought were the flags of the world in his *Book of Knowledge of All Kingdoms* recorded the gold tetragrammatic cross on red (he misunderstood the Bs and called them *links*), *quartered* with a red cross on white, as the flag of Constantinople (above left).[42] Although not usual, there are late Byzantine coins with this image too (above right).[43]

"The subject of Byzantine eagle motifs has fascinated many historical researchers during the course of the last century," wrote Anna Muthesius in 2004, "yet little consensus has been reached concerning their significance."[44] The literature is full of much debunking as later scholars point out that their predecessors' theories have been refuted, or relied on forgeries, or counted two heads on eagles where close examination revealed only one. This is likely the result of theorizing on the basis of insufficient data. Pseudo-Kodinos,

---

[39] The term comes from the Greek *tetragrammaton* [τετραγράμματον], meaning *four letters*. The word *tetragrammaton* in English is usually reserved for the four-letter name of the Hebrew god YHWH.

[40] Soloviev (1935), note 6, 159, recites the authority for dating this translation from after the Empire. The misidentification of the Bs as fire-steels or briquets (*pyrekbolōn*, πυρεκβόλων) dates back at least to the mid-14th century treatise on *Offices* of the anonymous writer known as Pseudo-Kodinos. See the text in Jean Verpeaux, ed., *Pseudo-Kodinos: Traité des Offices* (Paris, 1966), Ch. III, line 21, p. 167. An English translation has just been published: see Ruth Macrides *et al.*, *Pseudo-Kodinos and the Constantinopolitan Court: Offices and Ceremonies* (Farnham [England], 2013).

[41] As shown by Babuin, note 31.

[42] *El Libro del conoscimiento de todos los reinos*, a manuscript of the last quarter of the 14th century. It was the first illustrated flag book anywhere. An English translation was published by the Hakluyt Society as Clements Markham, ed., *Book of the Knowledge...*, Second Series, No. 29 (London, 1912). The discussion of Constantinople appears there at p. 55, and this image at plate 17, no. 82. See also the modern bilingual version by Nancy F. Marino, ed., *El Libro del conoscimiento de todos los reinos*, Medieval and Renaissance Texts and Studies [Arizona Studies in the Middle Ages and Renaissance] (Tempe [Arizona], 1999), 198:94-95.

[43] The coin was issued by John V and Matthew Cantacuzene as co-emperors around 1350.

[44] Muthesius (2004), note 14, 227. She continues: "Some scholars have attempted to explain Byzantine eagles purely as 'heraldic devices' in the Western sense, treating the appearance of the Palaeologian double-headed eagle on imperial cloths in Byzantine miniatures of the thirteenth to fourteenth centuries as a parallel phenomenon to Western-style coats of arms. This, however, is to overlook the fact that Western-style 'heraldic symbolism' bore little relation to Byzantine material expressions of noble birth." *Ibid.*

our main authority on late Byzantine court ceremonial, is not much help, as he describes the uniforms of high officials, including their eagles, in great detail but never specifies that any such eagle was to have more than one head.[45] The existing materials do not allow a clear understanding of the exact role of the double eagle in Byzantine state or imperial symbolism.[46]

The use of western heraldic forms in Byzantium (or in the West to represent Byzantine figures or institutions) after the restoration of the Empire in 1261 would be a useful topic for future research. At the moment the scarcity of clear examples hampers our understanding. Architectural and monumental carvings like those in the 13th century Paragoritissa Church in Arta[47] (Figure 32), and the slab in Mistra marking the site of the coronation of Constantine XI in 1449 (Figure 33), have been well documented, but their exact meaning and status as heraldic emblems are still ambiguous. The focus of research should be on material objects in both East and West. Princess Tamar's locket is a superb example of a material object; the earring of Queen Maria [Palaeologina] of Serbia (Figure 34) is another. But how many others are there whose armorial markings have been overlooked or misunderstood?

 There is an uneasy consensus, which I join, that the Palaeologues used the double eagle at least as a *badge*, meaning here a representative device but not part of a developed heraldic system. But it seems more associated with the office of despot than with the emperor. And even as a badge of the dynasty, the double eagle took its place among others – the monogram, a lattice (the so-called "gaming square"), the cross-swastika, and others – see Figure 35.[48] The Palaeologue monogram, called a *sympilēma* [συμπίλημα], was composed of the Greek letters Π Α Λ Γ (P A L G) and was used on coins and extensively as a dynastic mark. Figure 36 shows the *sympilēma* in use on a

45   See Verpeaux, *Pseudo-Kodinos,* note 40, Chapter II (On the Uniforms of Dignities and Offices), pp. 141-166.

46   "In the final analysis, the eagle should be identified as a generalized symbol of empire or perhaps of rulership, perhaps associated with apotheosis – an emblem of power and not of a specific person or family." Robert Ousterhout, "Byzantium between East and West and the Origins of Heraldry," in Colum Hourihane, ed., *Byzantine Art: Recent Studies* [Arizona Studies in the Middle Ages and Renaissance (Tempe [Arizona], 2009), 33:153-170], 160.

47   Capital of the Greek Despotate of Epirus during and after the Latin ascendancy. This church was built by Nikephoras I Comnenus Doukas, a despot but not a Palaelogue, between 1294 and 1296. See Chotzakoglou, note 19, 64.

48   And see other examples in Ousterhout, note 46, 157-170.

double eagle.[49] Above: a coin of Manuel II, showing the *sympilēma* and the lattice. Ousterhout makes a good case that monograms rather than graphic images came the closest in function to the heraldic imagery of the West.[50]

The double eagle as a Palaeologue badge, and its association with certain court titles (especially despot), together account for its use by a variety of princes and dynasts, including the rulers of the Greek states of Epirus, Morea and Trebizond (set up during the Latin control of Constantinople). The connection to the bearer could be somewhat tenuous – Tamar Comnena's mother was a Palaeologue and her father, although a Doukas, was a despot in Epirus.[51] The Gattilusi, descendants of a Genoese adventurer given Aegean lands and a Palaeologue princess in 1355, made conspicuous use of both the double eagle and the Palaeologue monogram for more than 100 years thereafter (Figure 38). A Palaeologue connection was not uncommon in the high élite of late Byzantium – the aristocracy was intricately intermarried, and only they left relics adorned with eagles.[52] My purpose here is not to survey all the examples but to suggest that the eagle could (but need not) come along with Palaeologue connections and/or a high princely title. Our present state of knowledge does not really allow us to say more.

I feel obliged to mention a startling theory suggested by Donald Nicol. In 1316 Emperor Andronicus II Palaeologue, then 34 years into his reign, had his grandson Andronicus III crowned nominal co-emperor, but disinherited him in 1321. Andronicus III rebelled and in 1325, after an unpleasant civil war, compelled Andronicus II to accept him as joint ruler. "It was probably at this stage," writes Nicol,

> that the double-headed eagle first became the device of the house of Palaiologos, symbolizing not, as is often thought, a great empire that looked at once to east and

---

[49] This drawing, from Babuin, note 31, at 57, no. 86, gives the outline of an image, gold on red in life, that I have seen variously attributed to a church fresco, a prayer book of Demetrius Palaeologue, and a (possibly post-Byzantine) binding on the *Codex Sinaiticus*, now in St. Catherine's monastery in the Sinai. The image may have been used in more than one place. For a color image see Wikimedia Commons at tinyurl.com/pqy9joa.

[50] See Ousterhout, note 46, 162-3.

[51] Nicol (1996), note 37, 24.

[52] "Great families of the élite advertised their breeding and their wealth by making sure that their family names were known; and the mothers and wives of those families took to adopting strings of ... names ... By the fourteenth century the most well-born and influential families were those of Palaeologue and Cantacuzene; and by the fifteenth century almost everyone among the élite was related to one or the other." Nicol (1996), note 37, 3. He gives the example of the abbess Theodora Branaina Komnene Laskarina Cantacuzene Palaeologina. *Id.*, 4. In such a world a lot of people were Palaeologues enough to display a double eagle badge.

west, but a sordid division of imperial authority between two disputatious emperors of the same family.[53]

As distinguished a historian as Nicol was, I feel this cannot be right. First, the double eagle was in use in imperial circles well before 1325 – Princess Tamar's locket, for example, is dated to 1294. Also it seems unlikely that a dynastic device would deliberately commemorate so humiliating (and as Nicol says, sordid) a circumstance. And the joint reign of these two emperors only lasted three years – in 1328 Andronicus III forced his grandfather to abdicate and made him retire, "blind through tears,"[54] to a monastery. I doubt a symbol of this unwilling partnership would long have survived its dissolution, or that the loser in these circumstances would have displayed it on a banner in his monastery, as Andronicus II seems to have done.[55]

The double eagle does appear to have been a state emblem of Trebizond, a small state established on the southeastern shore of the Black Sea. It came under Comnenus rule at the time the Byzantine Empire was overthrown in 1204, and continued as a separate state until 1460. Figure 37 shows Emperor Manuel I of Trebizond (mid-13th century) in a double-eagle robe. But the very absence of such an image of any Byzantine emperor reinforces the conclusion that the double eagle was not so used there.

The clearest examples of the double eagle used to designate the Eastern emperor appear not in Byzantium but in the West. Thus Giovanni Villani (d. 1348) says in his *Nuova Cronica* [New Chronicle] that "Constantine and later other Greek emperors went back to Julius Caesar's arms of a golden eagle on a red field, but with two heads."[56] When the Italian artist Filarete depicted the journey of Emperor John VIII Palaeologue to the Council of Ferrara in 1438, he showed the cabin of his galley decorated with a double eagle.[57] The door panel is seen below; Figure 39 is a detail of the Emperor and his cabin.

---

[53]   Nicol (1979), note 13, 31.

[54]   Nicephoras Gregoras, *Roman History*, IX, 8, quoted in Herbert Adam Gibbons, *The Foundation of the Ottoman Empire …* (London, 1916), 59.

[55]   The double-eagle device on Andronicus II's banner may be seen in Hubert De Vries' article "Byzantium: Arms and Emblems," see note 35.

[56]   Quoted by Giuseppe Gerola, "L'aquila bizantina e l'aquila imperiale a due teste" [The Byzantine eagle and the imperial double eagle], *Felix Ravenna* (Faenza, 1934), 43:7-36, at 16 (tr. DFP). Of course Villani's attribution of arms to Julius Caesar is unhistorical.

[57]   See Soloviev (1935), note 6, 135. The Council of Ferrara attempted to reconcile the Roman and Orthodox churches. Antonio di Pietro Avellino (c. 1400 – c. 1469), called Filarete (Φιλάρετος, Greek for *lover of excellence*), rendered his design in bronze on the door of the old St. Peter's Basilica in Rome (the doors have been preserved in the present building). The door project was completed in 1445, only a few years after the Emperor's visit, so it *may* have been based on an

(footnote continues →)

In Florence in 1439 John VIII granted an Italian citizen a double-eagle *augmentation* to his arms, a practice not known in Constantinople.[58] It is perhaps telling that the emperor used his badge for this purpose and not the emblem of the state.

Conrad Grünenberg, in his *Armorial*, attributed double-eagle arms to the eastern emperor.[59] Spanish and Italian *portulanos* (sailing maps) indicate Trebizond and

---

(footnote continues ...)

eyewitness account. Indeed it is *possible* that Filarete saw the emperor at Ferrara – in 1438 he and his colleague Simone had already been employed on the door project for five years, and according to Vasari "were not always at work on the … door" during that time. Giorgio Vasari, *Lives of the Most Eminent Painters, Sculptors and Architects* (1550; edition consulted London, 1912-14), 2:4. Certainly John VIII and his outrageous hat look very much as they did in Pisanello's famous medal portrait, which we know was modeled from life (it can be seen on Wikimedia at tinyurl.com/nledafa). The double-eagle decoration of a Venetian state barge is attested in the *Chronicle* of the Greek historian George Phrantzes, who was very close to the Palaeologues. See Soloviev (1935), note 6, 135.

[58] See Cervodeanu, note 36, 414.

[59] *Das Wappenbuch Conrads von Grünenberg, Ritters und Bürgers zu Constanz* [Conrad of Grünenberg's armorial of the knights and citizens of Constance] (Augsburg, 1483). The word *Bürger* actually means more than *citizen*, implying at least middle-class status and some political rights beyond those of the mass of the city's residents. The work is digitized from the original in the Bayerische Staatsbibliothek [Bavarian state library], and appears on the website of the Münchener DigitalizierungZentrum [Munich digitalizing center], where the whole book can be seen, and images enlarged and captured, at tinyurl.com/mq7b835. The Constantinople page is frame 0077. Grünenberg also shows the tetragrammatic cross arms, the cross-and-ringed-crosslets arms favored by the Latin emperors, and another one, quite unhistorical: red with two yellow vertical stripes, and above them two gold crowns on blue (*gules two pallets or, on a chief azure two crowns proper*). Three pages later, at frame 00080, he depicts a rooster (!) as the arms of the Emperor of Trebizond. A modern critical edition of this work, in English (but without pictures), is available in pdf format on the Medieval Armorials website at tinyurl.com/kclad24.

(footnote continues →)

sometimes Byzantium and with double-eagle banners. A definitely Greek example, from after the fall of Constantinople, is the house mark of Zacharias Calliergi's Greek printing house in Venice, which began operations in 1499 (Figure 40).[60]

I have confined my comments to official and secular manifestations of the double eagle, omitting discussion of the eagle in the Church where it was in active use. I cannot resist, though, offering Figure 41, a magnificent double eagle banner, dating from 1363-84 and now restored to superb condition. It was long thought to be a military flag, but in fact it was a church banner commissioned by a prelate who, although not a Palaeologue, pretended he was.[61] It is the best example I know, and certainly the best on textile, of what a Byzantine double eagle really looked like (see details in Figures 42-3). The medallion on the eagle's breast states the prelate's name, his title and his supposed family.

THE EARLY HERALDIC PERIOD IN THE WEST

Heraldry in Western Europe began rather abruptly in the middle of the 12th century. Before that time shields were certainly decorated, but not with the personal, relatively permanent, hereditary emblems that characterize the European heraldic system.[62] For example in the Bayeux Tapestry, completed around 1070, warriors are shown with shields of

---

(footnote continues ...)

Parenthetical descriptions of coats of arms will be given in the language of blazon. The function of blazon is to provide a technical description of a coat of arms so precise that the arms can be reconstructed accurately without a picture. English blazon uses many Norman French words, including the words for colors, and can be hard to understand without prior study. It is a system that could use some reform. Nevertheless I have chosen to avoid ambiguity by rendering blazon in the traditional style, after a description in ordinary language.

[60] It was largely funded by Anna Notaras Palaeologina, a Byzantine *grande dame* in Venetian exile, who no doubt approved the design before it was used. See Nicol (1996), note 37, 106.

[61] For more on this banner, and the deceitful cleric, see Jennifer L. Ball, "A Double-Headed Eagle Embroidery: From Battlefield to Altar," *Metropolitan Museum Journal*, 41:59-64 (New York, 2006), and the companion article by Kathrin Colburn, "A Double-Headed Eagle Embroidery: Analysis and Conservation," *Metropolitan Museum Journal*, 41:65-74 (New York, 2006).

[62] Beryl Stubbs, in *Origins of Heraldry* (London, 1980), makes an argument for an earlier origin, and perhaps a survival of Carolingian forms, in Boulogne and Flanders. Even if true, this does not change the sequence or timing for Germany and the rest of Europe.

inconsistent patterns.[63] The same is true of the 12th century fresco in Gozzo Castle [*Gozzoburg*] in Krems, Austria (above). By 1150 some of the military class had moved toward consistency in shield decoration; the devices on their shields were thought of more as personal or even family symbols and were continued by the next generation. There is no absolute starting date for this new identification system, but the enameled brass tomb plate of Geoffroi V Plantagenet, Count of Anjou (1149), is a traditional landmark in the process.[64] After that date we can ordinarily (although not always) regard shield decoration in Western Europe as heraldic.

It has become traditional to say that the Crusades were catalytic in the creation of Western heraldry. No doubt they were the most important military development for a couple of generations before and after 1150. And no doubt some Crusaders did come into contact with a quasi-heraldic system in the Moslem territories, especially Egypt.[65] Certainly before the Crusades there was no heraldry, and by the time they were halfway done there was. But no causal connection has ever been demonstrated.

The *single*-headed eagle was a frequent motif in European decorative art long before heraldry, indeed since antiquity.[66] The tenth century brooch of Gisela of Swabia (Figure 44) is a typical pre-heraldic example. The *double* eagle began appearing in Western art well before the beginning of heraldry. The earliest example I have found is from a manuscript called *Clementis papae I Recognitiones* [Recognitions of Pope Clement I], by an anonymous monk of Mont St.-Michel in France around 1000.[67] We have already seen

---

[63] The Bayeux Tapestry, really an embroidery, is a close-to-contemporary record of the Norman invasion and conquest of England in 1066. It is on display in the Musée de la Tapisserie [Tapestry museum] in Bayeux in Normandy. It can be seen digitally on the website of the Bibliotheca Augustana in Augsburg, at tinyurl.com/3pvmnbn.

[64] The plate was made for his tomb in Le Mans Cathedral in Normandy. A digital image can be seen on Wikimedia Commons at tinyurl.com/k4oyd7f.

[65] This system, used mostly in glass, ceramics, and stone carving, is called in Europe *Saracenic* heraldry, from the medieval Christian word for *Moslems*. Any influence it may have had on the origin of western heraldry is undocumented. For more on Saracenic heraldry see, e.g., William Leaf and Sally Purcell, *Heraldic Symbols: Islamic Insignia and Western Heraldry* (London, 1986). The standard work is Mayer, see note 7.

[66] A powerful bird of prey, not always an eagle, is an important motif in the art and folklore of many societies.

[67] Now in the Municipal Library in Avranches, France. See Androudis (2013), note 9, 218. In the illumination, available digitally in Androudis' paper at tinyurl.com/oy6wpkm, a two-headed eagle stands between arches that frame the Archangel Michael (killing a devil) and a monk. I am grateful to Hubert de Vries for pointing out this image, which may be seen in the article "Two-Headed Eagle" on his Hubert-Herald website, cited in note 6.

many instances of the double eagle in architectural details of French Romanesque buildings of the 11th century – see Figures 23-27.[68]

The double eagle had considerable currency in Germany in the early heraldic period. We know it was used for some purposes by the Babenberg Dukes of Austria in the 12th century, although perhaps not as a heraldic emblem.[69] Duke Leopold IV (1136-41) minted a silver penny at Krems with a double eagle design (Figure 45).[70] Figure 46 is a double eagle wall tile, dated to the mid-12th century, from St. Emmeram's Abbey Church in Regensberg where some of the Babenberg family were buried.[71]

The earliest *definitely heraldic* double eagle I have been able to find in Western Europe, from 1185, is seen in Figure 47 on a seal of Count Ludwig von Sarwarden. Note its characteristically Eastern shape, with both heads on one neck, distinct from the two-necked heraldic style that emerged later. The eagle's breastshield is decorated in the pre-heraldic manner.[72] Figures 48 and 49 are 13th-century German seals.[73] None of these are imperial uses, but show the currency of the image in Germany in proto- and early heraldic times.[74]

---

[68]   Androudis (2013), note 9, 219-223. Androudis regards all of them as based on Spanish Islamic patterns. *Id.*, 224.

[69]   The Babenbergs, a dynasty now long extinct, were lords of Austria before the Hapsburgs – the Austrian arms, a white horizontal stripe on red (*gules, a fess argent*), were originally theirs.

[70]   Figure 45 actually shows a later example, minted by Leopold V around 1197, because it is a much cleaner strike of more or less the same design. For images of the earlier coin, see the AC Search coin website at tinyurl.com/mpduy2l. Leopold VI issued similar coins at Vienna and Enns c. 1210-30; so did Ulrich III of Kärnten in the mid-13th century.

[71]   The tile is dated to around 1175. See Anna Pawlik, "Ornament und Eleganz" [Ornament and elegance], from the German National Museum's publication KulturGut (Nuremberg, 2013), no. 37. p. 2, fig. 2, on the museum's website at tinyurl.com/qaunjdh. Compare the 13th century Hungarian cloak fastener at Figure 198.

[72]   By the time this eagle appears for Sarwarden in the French *Armorial Bellenville*, dated around the end of the 14th century, it has two separate necks in the usual Western style, and no breastshield. See the facsimile of page 18r in Léon Jequier, *L'Armorial Bellenville* (Paris, 1983), 266, and his note on the dating (under the heading "16. Cologne") in *ibid.*, 19.

[73]   The seal of Poppo of Henneberg (Figure 48) may share a connection with the Bavarian examples – the Counts of Henneberg and the (Babenberg) Dukes of Austria were (or claimed to be) descendants of a Frankish dynasty called the House of Poppo. Leopold V's mother Theodora Comnena was a Byzantine princess, and so were the wives of his son and grandson.

[74]   References to other early uses may be found in, e.g., John Woodward and George Burnett, *Treatise on Heraldry British and Foreign* (London, 1891-96), 251-2 (modern reprint Rutland [Vermont], 1969). A number of others are usefully collected and illustrated in Friedrich Karl von Hohenlohe-Waldenburg [Prince Hohenlohe], *Zur Geschichte der Heraldischer Doppeladler* [On

(footnote continues →)

31

In 476, as mentioned, the Western part of the Roman Empire fell to the Germanic warlord Odoacer.[75] In 800 Pope Leo III and the Frankish king Charles the Great (called Charlemagne) nominally revived the Western Empire by arranging for Charles to be crowned as emperor.[76] This Carolingian Empire (so called after Charles (= Karl, Latin *Carolus*), and his grandfather Charles Martel who established the dynasty, perished due to partitions and political weakness, but was revived and refounded in 962 by the Saxon Otto I, and continued in theory until 1806.

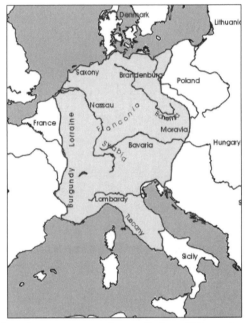

This second try at a supposedly revived Western Empire, later called the *Holy Roman Empire* and the *Roman Empire of the German Nation*, included in theory all of Germany and half of Italy, as well as other territories such as Bohemia, Burgundy and parts of the Low Countries. The map at right shows the approximate extent of the Empire in 1190; over the centuries the emperor's deteriorating claim to overlordship in Italy became a subject of constant conflict and debilitating warfare. At the start of the heraldic period the Empire, although theoretically elective, was more or less hereditary in the Swabian House of Hohenstaufen, the latest of a series of German dynasties to hold that distinction.

The landmark early representation of the double eagle as the arms of a Western emperor is found in the manuscript of the *Historia Anglorum* [History of the English] by the English monk Matthew Paris, where it is shown as the arms of Frederick II, emperor from 1220 to 1250.[77] See Figure 50. It is hard to tell,

---

(*footnote continues ...*)

the history of the heraldic double eagle] (Stuttgart, 1871), digitized by the Münchener DigitalisierungsZentrum of the Bayerische Staatsbibliothek [Bavarian state library] and available on their website at tinyurl.com/p9jv8gg.

[75]   Some think Odoacer might have been a Hun rather than a German. He was the first of a long series of "barbarian" Kings of Italy.

[76]   The idea called *translatio imperii* [transfer of the empire], favored by contemporary theorists of history and western apologists for successive emperors, held that sacred character of the Roman Empire was transmitted in linear fashion to the Western Empire established by Charlemagne and revived by Otto.

[77]   The autograph manuscript of volume III of this work, containing the pages about Frederick II, is in the British Library. The whole book can be seen, and images enlarged and captured, on the

(*footnote continues →*)

at this remove, whether these arms really were used by Frederick as an imperial heraldic emblem. Paris was one of the most engaging of medieval artists, but for all his skill and charm was not always the most reliable chronicler.[78] The colors black and gold are suggestive, though – they might have been taken by Frederick from his dynastic (Hohenstaufen) arms of three black lions on gold (*or, three lions passant sable*), which lends support to their authenticity. Paris shows variants of these arms in use by three of Frederick's sons: Conrad, Manfred and Anso [Enzo].[79] If differenced versions of the double eagle were indeed borne by Frederick's sons, two of whom (Manfred and Anso) were illegitimate, that would suggest a device more personal than imperial, a conclusion consistent with the argument from the colors.[80]

If Frederick II (left) did actually use the double eagle as a personal device, it seems more likely that he adapted it from Byzantine or Islamic usage than that he made this figure up from his imagination.[81] Of all the rulers of western Europe during this period, Frederick, with his seat in Sicily, his visit to Syria and Jerusalem in 1228-29, his commercial and intellectual engagement with the whole of the former Roman world, and his inclusive cultural vision, was the most likely to be familiar with Byzantine and Islamic usage. Frederick did not himself use the double eagle on any seal

---

(footnote continues ...)

British Library's website at tinyurl.com/og97g93. The relevant page (149r) shows a black double eagle on gold, reversed for the Emperor's death. (Pages in manuscripts are customarily noted as *r* for *recto* [front] and *v* for *verso* [back].) It seems fair to date this page around 1258.

[78] For an attractive modern sampler of Paris' writing, generously illustrated in color with his charmingly clear drawings, see Richard Vaughan, ed., *The Illustrated Chronicles of Matthew Paris* (Cambridge, 2d ed. 1993). The shield of Frederick II is illustrated, with its accompanying text, at 198.

[79] Paris has Conrad [IV of Germany, I of Sicily, II of Jerusalem] (1228-1254) bearing a black double eagle on gold with a curious red dotted crescent between its heads. *Historia Anglorum* at 164v. At 165v he shows Manfred (1232-1266), King of Sicily from 1258, bearing the same black double eagle on gold, without the crescent but with a silver stripe laid horizontally over it (*or, a double eagle sable, overall a fess argent*); at 145v he shows Anso with the left half of the golden field in green (*per pale vert and or, a double eagle sable*). Anso's shield can be see in close-up view on Wikimedia Commons at tinyurl.com/lycdnhb.

[80] When Manfred became King of Sicily in succession to his father, his coins bore a single-headed eagle.

[81] This portrait of Frederick, from a medallion in a church in Calabria, may not be an accurate representation.

or coin.[82] Instead he used the single-headed eagle (known as the *Reichsadler*), and indeed his *augustalis*, one of the most famous and beautiful gold coins of the Middle Ages, intended as a showpiece, had an eagle with only one head (Figure 51).[83]

Except for this ambiguous supposed use by Frederick II, no Western emperor or German king used the double eagle as an imperial emblem on a coin or seal for generations after his death in 1250.[84] The ordinary single-headed eagle had been the arms of Germany

---

[82] As noted, a series of double-eagle coins was minted *for him* in at the Sicilian mint in Messina in 1202-03, during his minority, See Figure 18. But these were not imperial issues, as Frederick did not become emperor until 1220. For a large array of the coins of Frederick II, see the Coin-archives website page at tinyurl.com/mdl5a8t.

[83] The word *Reichsadler* is difficult to translate. *Adler* means eagle, but *Reich* means *empire*, and also (until after World War II) the German dominion or domain in whatever form or extent it might be imagined, even if not called an empire. So it would be both correct and misleading to translate *Reichsadler* as *imperial eagle* or *eagle of the empire*. It was (and indeed still is) the emblem of Germany. And it was the emblem of the German king whether he was also emperor or not. The Weimar Republic, and Hitler's Germany that succeeded it, neither one formally an empire, were both called *Deutsches Reich*. Hitler's slogan *Ein Reich, Ein Volk, Ein Führer* [one *Reich*, one people, one leader] shows the ambiguity of the word – did *Reich* mean state, or government, or nation, or dominion, or imperial aspiration, or just what? Today the *Reichsadler* is carefully called the *Bundesadler* [federal eagle], in Austria as well as Germany, to show discontinuity with the bad old days.

[84] Otto IV (reigned 1198-1218) did mint one coin (Figure 52) with a lion on the obverse and a double eagle (in the old single-necked style) on the reverse. See Heinrich Philipp Cappe, *Die Münzen der deutschen Kaiser und Könige des Mittelalters* [The coins of the German emperors and kings of the Middle Ages] (3 vols., Dresden, 1848-57), 1:154 (no. 692) and plate 22 (no. 368). It is the only one of the hundreds Cappe lists as struck between 1100 and 1400 to bear a double eagle at all.

Otto Posse (1847-1921) collected all the known seals of the German kings and emperors in his magisterial five-volume *Die Siegel der Deutschen Kaiser und Könige: von 751 bis 1806* [The seals of the German emperors and kings from 751 to 1806] (Dresden, 1909-13), available in facsimile through Wikimedia Commons at tinyurl.com/mcmsv6r. I am relying on his collection as comprehensive; if he missed a seal it would be an outlier. Even the so-called Golden Bull (issued to seal the decree of Emperor Charles IV in 1356, reorganizing the procedure for electing an emperor), familiarly identified by its seal (Latin *bulla*), carried the single-headed eagle. An image of this famous seal appears on Wikimedia Commons at tinyurl.com/mjox2b6.

There is a seal of Empress Maria, widow of Otto IV, from 1258, that shows half an eagle with one complete head. See Gustav Seyler, *Geschichte der Heraldik* [History of heraldry] (Nuremberg, 1890; modern reprint Neustadt an der Asch, 1970), 282, fig. 369. But because the two heraldic fields of this seal are *dimidiated* (that is, split vertically in half before being joined together), rather than *impaled* (the joined figures shown complete in each field after joining), as became the later practice, the eagle could as easily be single-headed, and given the period and the context that's what I think it is.

since earliest heraldic times. It was also the sign of the Empire and the emperor, as well as that of the original *Roman* emperors and Empire, carried by every Roman legion since Marius and carved in countless monuments all over the ancient world.[85] And it was the arms of the "King of the Romans," the imperial title given to a German king when he was chosen emperor-elect by the prince-electors.[86] The King of the Romans was expected in due course also to be crowned King of Italy (at Pavia, with the Iron Crown of Lombardy), and to assume the title of emperor after he had been crowned *personally by the Pope*.[87] A papal coronation was traditionally required before the title of emperor [*Kaiser*] could officially be used.[88]

King Wenceslaus IV of Bohemia, called in German *Wenzel der Faule* [Wenceslaus the Idle], was never emperor. But in 1363, at the age of two, he was appointed King of Bohemia by his father, Emperor Charles IV, who held the same title.[89] At this time a seal was issued for him (certainly with the emperor's approval) showing a double eagle with the two-tailed lion of Bohemia on a breastshield (Figure 53). When his father died in 1378, Wenceslaus became the German king in his place and was elected King of the Romans. In the course of a difficult reign King Wenceslaus never became emperor, and was deposed as King of the Romans in 1400. But in 1396 he issued another double eagle

---

[85]   Pliny the Elder, in his *Natural History* (book 10, chapter 5.4), recites that Gaius Marius, leader of the Roman Republic, made the eagle the emblem of all the Roman legions during his second term as consul (105 BC). Before that, although the eagle ranked first, some divisions carried a wolf, a minotaur, a horse or a wild boar instead. See text on Tufts University's Perseus Digital Library website at tinyurl.com/mk9mjly.

[86]   The original seven electors were the Archbishops of Mainz, Trier and Cologne (all Roman-founded cities), the Duke of Saxony, the Margrave of Brandenburg, the Count Palatine of the Rhine, and the King of Bohemia. The composition of this college of prince-electors (*Kurfürsten*) changed slightly over the long history of the Empire. Their votes for the King of the Romans were usually secured by enormous bribes.

[87]   Indeed the Golden Bull of 1356, issued by the imperial Diet [Assembly], referred to the German King as *rex in imperatorem promovendus* [the king to be promoted emperor]. The delay between election and coronation could be many years. Charles V was the last emperor to be crowned by the Pope, in 1530. On the Iron Crown itself, see note 176 below.

[88]   The German word *Kaiser*, like the Russian word *Tsar*, is derived from the name of Caesar (pronounced in Latin with a hard C).

[89]   They were of the dynasty of Luxemburg. It was not unusual in medieval times for a king to promote and even crown a son or other heir during his own reign. The usual purpose was not to associate the younger king in actual rule, but to assure the succession. This King Wenceslaus was not the one in the Christmas carol – that was St. Wenceslaus I, Duke of Bohemia (907-935).

seal, as King of Bohemia, of similar design to that of 1363. These were the first such seals known for any member of a Western imperial family.[90]

We do not know why these seals were cut with the double eagle. Perhaps the second seal was intended the show that Wenceslaus was King of Germany and of the Romans *as well* as of Bohemia, to emphasize his dignity in the absence of the imperial title.[91] But that does not explain why this design was chosen for him in 1363, when he was only a child and not king either of Germany or of the Romans. Whatever it meant, it could not have been used as an imperial emblem as he was never emperor – indeed there was an imperial interregnum throughout Wenceslaus' reign, from the death of Charles IV in 1378 until Sigismund's coronation in 1434.

When Wenceslaus was deposed as King of the Romans in 1400[92] he was succeeded by Rupert, the Elector Palatine. In 1402, during Rupert's reign, Wenceslaus' half-brother Sigismund (left) used a double eagle seal in his role as imperial vicar (a sort of viceroy, an imperial office).[93] When Rupert died in 1410, Sigismund was elected King of the Romans, and in 1417 ordered a beautiful imperial seal for himself, also with a double eagle (Figure 54). The Latin text of the original order to the seal-cutter survives, so we know the double eagle was chosen deliberately to be Sigismund's imperial emblem at that time. No doubt he planned to be crowned soon.[94]

But as it turned out, he was not crowned Emperor until 1433, 16 years later. He began using the seal in 1434. So it is a question whether the double eagle became the official emblem of the Empire in 1417, when Sigismund ordered the seal, or 1433 when he became Emperor, or 1434 when he began using the seal. However that may be decided, it is fair to say that the formal official symbolic use of the double eagle by the Western

---

90 The first such seals known to Posse, anyway – see note 84. Another double-eagle seal was issued for Wenceslaus in 1371 – see *id.*, vol. 2, plate 7, no. 4.

91 Gerola suggests unpersuasively, note 56, at 34, that it was a graphic combination of the eagles of Silesia and Brandenburg.

92 For the first time; he was deposed *again* in 1402 before finally getting the hint and abdicating under pressure in 1411.

93 The portrait of Sigismund, attributed to Pisanello, is notable for the size of the imperial earmuffs.

94 The Latin text appears in Posse, note 84, vol. 5, p. 47.

emperors dates from Sigismund's reign, and was continuous thereafter until the end of the Empire.[95]

But we should not regard his reign as a firm boundary – one head before, two after – the way a modern statute or flag regulation changes legalities at a stroke. The situation in the 14th and 15th centuries was more fluid than that. Well before Sigismund's reign, for example, when a city obtained a charter and became a free imperial city, it often placed its arms on the breast of a double eagle.[96] The single eagle on the seal of Friedberg, borne in 1260, became a double eagle by 1344 (compare Figures 55 and 56). There is no doubt that these seals were intended to allude to the emperor from whom Friedberg's charter derived. Kaiserswerd had a double eagle seal in the time of Emperor Frederick II, and even put his name into the inscription (Figure 57).

The same process was followed in the arms of other cities, like Vienna, and even some outside the German language area.[97] Groningen in the Netherlands, for instance, began to use a single-headed eagle as a supporter for its arms when it became an imperial city; after Sigismund's coronation the eagle grew another head.[98] Figure 58 is the medieval city banner of Cologne. Figure 59 is the double eagle seal of the Jewish community in Augsburg (1298), incorporated under imperial protection in an imperial city.[99]

Before Sigismund, the German King was understood to bear a single-headed eagle, whether he had been crowned emperor or not. This may be seen in the major heraldic works of the period. For example, the *Zürich Wappenrolle*, around 1340, shows the

---

[95]   Sigismund issued two coins where the double eagle appeared, quite small, as a sort of mint mark, between the feet of a saint, where similar coins have an initial letter or a crescent moon. See Cappe, note 84, 2:131 (no. 605) and 3:157 (no. 699). But not until Frederick III, who succeeded him as emperor in 1452, are there imperial coins with a double eagle as a central image. See *id.*, 1:181-2 (nos. 834-6) and plate 16 (nos. 270-1), and the text figure on page 8 above.

[96]   Many cities in the Empire were so-called *free* or *imperial cities*, meaning they had been granted imperial charters and so stood in direct relations with the Emperor, out of the control of intermediate feudal lords or church authorities. This was part of the alliance, repeated all over Europe, between the crown and the rising cities against the magnates.

[97]   Vienna was granted the double eagle, in place of its earlier single eagle, as a concession by Frederick III in 1461. See Peter Diem, "Die Symbole Wiens" [Symbols of Vienna], on the Austria Forum website at tinyurl.com/lx27uma. For images of its seals before and after this change, see the Vienna page of the Historic Waxcraft website at tinyurl.com/o6anmzb.

[98]   Images of both eagles, from the Martinuskerk in Groningen, appear in Hubert de Vries, *Wapens van de Nederland* [Arms of the Netherlands] (Amsterdam, 1995), 116.

[99]   Note, between the eagle's heads, instead of a crown, the *Judenhut* [Jewish hat], required for German Jews and used in iconography as a distinguishing mark of a Jew.

Reichsadler for the Emperor: a black single-headed eagle on gold.[100] The mid-fourteenth century *Balduineum* shows Emperor Henry VII on his way to Rome with a single-headed eagle banner.[101] A miniature illustrating Giovanni Villani's *Nuova Cronica*, also of the mid-fourteenth century, shows the same for Frederick II in the Battle of Giglio.[102] *Gelre's Armorial*, from shortly before 1400, shows the single-headed eagle with the addition of a thin red border around the outside of the shield, which is certainly an artist's embellishment.[103] The miniature of Emperor Frederick VI in the *Grosser Heidelberger Liederhandscrift* [Great Heidelberg song manuscript] (right; around 1400), one of the greatest armorial monuments of the Middle Ages, shows for him a single-headed *Reichsadler* with the same ornamental red border in *Gelre*.[104] The *Armorial de Huldenberg* (1408-16) shows the same.[105]

---

[100]   Cf., e.g., Heinrich Runge, *Die Wappenrolle von Zürich* (Zürich, 1860), plate 1, no. 12 (facsimile). For a photographic facsimile of the original manuscript, with scholarly commentary in English, see Steen Clemmensen, *The Zürich Armorial* (2009), on pdf at <u>tinyurl.com/mgle2qn</u> (emperor's arms at 7).

[101]   *Balduineum* is the short title for the *Bilderzyklus des Codex Balduini Trevirensis* [Picture-cycle of the book of Baldwin of Treves]. Henry's trip to Rome began in 1310, but he didn't get there until 1312. The manuscript dates from considerably later. A digital facsimile of the *Balduineum* may be seen on the Rheinland-Pfalz Landesarchiv [State archive] website at <u>tinyurl.com/l9zstlm</u>, called there *Kaiser Heinrich's Romfahrt* (Emperor Henry's journey to Rome).

[102]   See image in Wikimedia Commons, at <u>tinyurl.com/mg995nx</u>. The Battle of Giglio was fought in 1241 but the manuscript dates from about 100 years later.

[103]   Cf. the facsimile of p. 26v in Jan van Helmont, ed., *Gelre* (Louvain, 1992), 81, with blazon and commentary at 291.

[104]   Cf. the reproduction in Elmar Mittler and Wilfried Werner, *Codex Manesse* (Heidelberg, 1988), 514, at plate E 5/1.

[105]   Cf. the facsimile of page 1 in Jan van Helmont, ed., *Armorial de Huldenberg* (Louvain, 1994), plate 2.

Examples could be multiplied. None of these documents (or a representative sample of others of the same period) shows a double eagle for the emperor.[106] Perhaps more telling than any armorial, the *Adlerdalmatika*, a vestment made in 1330-40 specifically for Emperor Louis (Ludwig) IV (already crowned), is decorated with medallions of a single-headed eagle. It seems likely that if the double eagle had been an imperial emblem at this time the *Adlerdalmatika* would have used it rather than the single-headed version.[107]

Even after Sigismund, the King of the Romans bore a single-headed eagle, as can be seen in the elaborate armorial "AEIOU" page in the *Handregistratur*, an official book of privileges and charters that was the personal property of Frederick III. It is clearly dated 1449, some years after his election as King of the Romans in 1440 but before his coronation as emperor in 1452.[108]

---

[106]   I am grateful for the list of medieval armorial manuscripts, with estimated dates, in Egon Freiherr von Berchem, D. L. Galbreath and Otto Hupp, *Beiträge zur Geschichte der Heraldik* [Contributions to the history of heraldry] (Berlin, 1939), a peerless conspectus of the manuscript literature. Where they give dates for manuscripts in their chronology, at 220, I have accepted their dates in my mention of these works.

   Even the sumptuous *Grand Armorial of the Golden Fleece* shows the Emperor decked out with armorial surcoat and caparison for his horse, both bearing a single-headed eagle. While the date of this armorial is not exactly fixed, the Order of the Golden Fleece was not founded until 1430, so the image certainly comes after that. Sigismund at that time had long been King of the Romans and emperor-elect, but the image of the emperor, whether Sigismund or some ideal emperor, still gets only one head on his eagle. The original of this work (*Grand Armorial de la Toison d'Or*) is in the Bibliothèque de l'Arsenal [Arsenal library] in Paris (Ms. 4790). A beautifully clear digitization is available on the library's website at tinyurl.com/m7pc8xa.

   Of course medieval manuscripts sometimes get things totally wrong. The *Wappenbuch "Von der Ersten"* of around 1380 attributes a plain gold shield (*or plein*) to the Western Emperor, and to the Eastern Emperor a shield divided vertically between plain gold and three red bulls' heads on white (*per pale, or plein and argent three bulls' heads caboshed gules horned or*). Both are of course utterly fanciful. See the facsimile *Wappenbuch von der Ersten*, edited by A. M. Hildebrandt (Berlin, 1893), 41r.

[107]   The *Adlerdalmatika* is in the Secular Treasury (*Weltliche Schatzkammer*) in the Imperial Palace in Vienna. An image may be seen on Wikimedia Commons at tinyurl.com/mfrvdy7. There are many early depictions of double eagle vestments used in Constantinople, and by medieval Serbian princes clearly robed in the Byzantine tradition. See Figures 37 and 161 and accompanying text and notes.

[108]   The AEIOU page from Frederick's *Handregistratur* (1449) is in the Haus-, Hof- und Staatsarchiv [House, court and state archives], Vienna. It can be seen on the website of the Austrian kult.docu project at tinyurl.com/l7vznnp. The sequence AEIOU was a motto of the House of Habsburg for which many meanings have been given, including *Austriae est imperare orbi universo* [Austria is given the whole world to rule] and *Alles Erdreich ist Oesterreich unterthan* (meaning roughly the same thing in German).

Despite exceptions, though, Emperor Sigismund's great seal of 1434 changed the convention, and from then forward the double eagle *did* signify the emperor, and the Empire, while the single-headed *Reichsadler* continued to stand for Germany, the German king, and his title of King of the Romans. The double eagle appeared on imperial seals, and on rescripts and other documents, and public buildings, and everywhere the emperor wished to make a public or even private display. Figure 61 is an image of the imperial flag, from a woodcut of 1545 – it is the black double eagle on gold, with a breastshield of Austria and Burgundy (see pages 45-47 below).[109] After the change in the imperial seals, the coins of the Empire also often bore the double eagle. Figure 60 shows typical coins of imperial cities from the reign of Charles V in the mid-16th century.[110] The imperial double eagle appears on the obverse of these coins, and the city's own arms appear on the reverse.[111]

Note a special crown above the eagle's head on the coins in Figure 60. In the top coin the crown has one arch and a miter-like structure on each side; in the middle coin it has two arches. These were heraldic crowns for the emperor only, inspired by (but not exactly following) the single-arched crown (called the *Bügelkrone* or hooped crown, see Figure 63), made for the emperors in Ottonian times but attributed to Charlemagne. Figure 64 shows the crown of Frederick III, who died in 1493, as it appears on his tomb; it has a hoop, and also a miter to show the sacred character of his office.

The Emperor and the German king were usually the same person, who bore the arms of both offices, and he is often shown with both in the graphic art of the period. Figure 65 is an image of Emperor Sigismund from Ulrich von Richenthal's *Chronik des Constanzer*

---

[109]   Thanks to Michael Göbl, whose essay "Propaganda in den Wappen der Habsburger Monarchie" [Propaganda in the arms of the Habsburg monarchy], on the Austrian Oktogon forum website at tinyurl.com/m9fl2at, first made me aware of this image.

[110]   The image is a detail from a larger image in John Porteous, *Coins in History* (New York, 1969). No specific attribution is given by Porteous, but the caption reads: "A sample of thalers issued by the free imperial cities of Germany in the mid-sixteenth century. A page of woodcuts from a traders' handbook showing all the types of thaler current in the Franconian, Swabian and Bavarian circles." The "circles" were a form of geographical arrangement for an empire too complex in constitution, and whose parts had been too fractured by dynastic subdivision, to allow for simple boundaries. The thaler (cognate to English *dollar*) was the standard silver coin of Germany. Charts like these (showing large numbers of sample coins) were used by money-changers to help them know what they were dealing with in the profusion of local issues, many of different fineness, weight and value. The specimens in Figure 60 were issued by Regensburg, Nuremberg and Lübeck.

[111]   Sometimes the city arms were set on a breastshield – see for example the arms of Lübeck in Figure 62, a modern boundary marker at the city line.

Konzils [Chronicle of the Council of Constance].[112] By 1480, when this image was created, it did not matter iconographically that the Council of Constance was held before Sigismund had been crowned Emperor – the *idea of the Empire* still merited a double eagle.

Observe that the imperial crown in Richenthal's design, although without a miter, has several arches, which the other crown does not have – before the Renaissance, closed crowns were not worn by ordinary kings. Richenthal's imperial eagle also displays a halo or *nimbus* (German *Heiligenschein* [light of holiness]) as a sign of its sacred character. Both these elements – the nimbus and the arched crown – were *attributes*, although not invariable ones, of the imperial double eagle.[113] Sometimes the eagle had royal crowns on its heads, with an imperial crown between them; this practice could be seen as emphasizing the Emperor's royal titles (Germany, Italy, Bohemia, Hungary and others).

More research is needed on the questions just when, how and why the double eagle came to represent the idea of the Empire. That it did so in the 13th century is obvious from the change in the seals of imperial cites, already mentioned.[114] But nevertheless (if the case of Frederick II is laid aside, as it probably should be) the emperors before Sigismund did not use it, with very rare exceptions, on their seals or coins or elsewhere. How then did the identification of the double eagle with the German/Roman imperial title come about? It *could* have been inspired by the double eagle badge of the Palaeologues, but there is no evidence that it *was* so inspired.

One possibility lies in the coinage of Baldwin II of Flanders (who became the first Latin Emperor in 1204), and his daughter Marguerite, called *of Constantinople* although she

---

[112]   The Council of Constance, held in 1414-18, was a church ecumenical council under Sigismund's presidency, called to resolve the absurd situation of three popes all claiming to reign at the same time. Richenthal's book, dating from 1480 and so not a contemporary record, was one of the most important heraldic manuscripts of the 15th century, and became even more important when a version made from woodcuts was printed in Augsburg in 1483, the first printed heraldic book. For a modern facsimile see Richard Michael Buck, ed., *Ulrich von Richenthal: Chronik des Constanzer Conzils* (Leipzig, 1936), or the digitalized facsimile on the Heidelberg University website at tinyurl.com/lyftvy8. Richenthal also gave arched crowns to the imagined arms of other supposed empires, for example Ethiopia and Tartary.

[113]   An *attribute* is an iconographic element in a composition that aids the viewer in identifying a subject in a composition, or communicates information about it.

[114]   There were other transitional forms – for instance Gerola, note 56, at 31-33, mentions a miniature of 1329 with the double-eagle arms, and some small figures on electoral coinage. It is in the nature of transitional forms to leave scant traces.

did not live or rule there. Baldwin did not use the double eagle on his seal as emperor,[115] and there are no surviving armorial coins from the Latin Empire.[116] But back in Flanders he and his daughter did issue double eagle coins – see Figure 66 for a coin of Marguerite's from 1244.[117] It could not have been a sign of imperial power, as Marguerite was never associated with the imperial throne or administration.[118] We may therefore *speculate* that the double eagle was adopted with the message: *we rule here, and we rule there also*. The early date of this Flemish coinage makes it a *possible* inspiration for the association of the image with the similarly double title of the German king-emperor in the seals of the imperial cities. If a document can be found in some dusty Flemish archive, indicating what Baldwin and Marguerite were thinking when they approved this design and ordered their coins, it could settle an enduring mystery.[119]

There is another possibility, also *entirely speculative*, that the identification of the double eagle with empire arose not from isolated images or coins or textiles but from the long and wide-ranging visit of Emperor Manuel II Palaeologue to Western Europe at the start of the 15th century. He traveled to France, Italy and even England in the years 1400-02, searching for political support.[120] It is at least *possible* that, as John VIII would later do in Ferrara, he displayed the double-eagle badge on his travels – on his clothes, carriage and horse-trappings, on the liveries of his servants, and elsewhere. The timing is right –

---

[115]   See the record of seals in Gustave Schlumberger, *Sceaux et Bulles des Empereurs Latins de Constantinople* [Seals of the Latin emperors of Constantinople] (Caen, 1980), available digitally at tinyurl.com/px4h3tk. A *bulla* is a seal impression in metal rather than wax.

[116]   See, e.g. Alan M. Stahl, "Coinage and Money in the Latin Empire," Dumbarton Oaks Papers, No. 55 (Washington, 2001), available digitally at tinyurl.com/mhavjn8.

[117]   The double eagle image was very influential among descendants of Baldwin and Marguerite, and spread widely among the local nobility in this early heraldic period. Gerola, note 56, 23 n.1, names five local noble families who used the double eagle on their armorial seals in the period 1259-1313, citing Johann Theodor de Raadt, *Sceaux armoríes des Pays-Bas et des pays avoisinants* [Armorial seals of the Netherlands and neighboring countries] (Brussels, 1903). The image ramified as far as Savoy. Gerola at 22-3, and see pages 60-61 below.

[118]   Ousterhout says, note 46 at 160, that Baldwin's daughters adopted the double eagle emblem as a sign of imperial connection, but gives no evidence or reasoning.

[119]   Counts Henri II and III of Brabant issued deniers with a double eagle as early as 1235, without any imperial connection. But these were all issued at their mint at Haelen, a town which itself had double-eagle arms. See Alphonse de Witte, *Histoire Monetaire des Comtes de Louvain, Ducs de Brabant, et Marquis du Saint Empire Romain* [Monetary history of the Counts of Louvain, Dukes of Brabant and marquesses of the Holy Roman Empire] (Antwerp, 1804), 1:60-61, and plate 6, nos. 133-140, available digitally on the website of the Société Royale de Numismatique de Belgique [Royal numismatic society of Belgium] at tinyurl.com/nryenmk.

[120]   For more on the embassy of Manuel II, see John W. Barker, *Manuel II Palaeologus (1391-1425): A Study in Late Byzantine Statesmanship* (New Brunswick [New Jersey], 1969).

Sigismund was already King of Hungary and Bohemia, and an important power in the Western Empire at this time; he became King of the Romans in 1411 and ordered his famous imperial seal in 1417.[121] But Manuel II made a sorry spectacle in Western Europe, wandering from court to court in a fruitless and sometimes hopeless quest for support, his empire almost gone and continuing to crumble the whole time he was there. He did not offer an imperial example likely to inspire imitation. Still, he was extravagantly honored wherever he went in the West, and his title at least still had some prestige left, so it cannot be ruled out that his visit and incidental display of the double eagle (if any) were factors. More research would be welcome.

Perhaps the simplest explanation lies in the multiplicity of eagles. The single-headed eagle – along with the lion – was one of the most common figures in early heraldry. If a new emblem was desired to distinguish the imperial office from the sovereignty of Germany (already represented by the *Reichsadler*), some change to the figure itself was the obvious solution. This was a well-recognized process called *differencing* – an example has already been seen in the changes reportedly made to Frederick II's supposed double eagle arms by (or for) his sons (see page 33). A change in colors would not have registered on seals or coins. Adding a *brisure* or differencing mark, as in the arms of

Bertrand de Guesclin (text figure on page 81) or the seal of Heinrich von Kirkel (Figure 49), would have been in-appropriate as the imperial office ranked above the German (or Roman) kingship. Changing the form of the eagle itself provided a good solution, one well within customary heraldic norms. The royal arms of Bohemia, for example, certainly well known within the Empire, varied the familiar lion by giving him a double tail (see the example, at right, from the 14th century tomb of King Ottokar II).[122] The image of the two-headed eagle was current anyway in Europe of the time, as we have seen in Bavaria and France and Flanders and elsewhere, so why not add another head? The explanations later offered – the two heads standing for east and west, church and state, etc. – could have been poetic justifications for the differencing rather than originating causes. This simplest of all explanations seems to me most likely to be the true one.

---

[121]   To have mattered, any influence would have had to come before 1417, and it would not account for the strange use of the double eagle on Wenceslaus' Bohemian seal, or Sigismund's Hungarian vicar's seal; but it might have been a factor in the imperial seal.

[122]   King Ottokar II died in 1278; his tomb (by the architect and sculptor Peter Parler) is in St. Vitus' Cathedral in Prague. These arms survive as an element of the arms of the Czech Republic.

One head, two heads? Why not three heads? Conrad Grünenberg, another chronicler of the Council of Constance, suggested this in his influential 1483 heraldic manuscript *Wappenbuch Grünenburg* [Grünenberg's Armorial].[123] With a medieval fondness for systematization, Grünenberg theorized: if one head is for the King of Germany, and two heads are for the more important office of the emperor, why not have *three* heads when the emperor fills both offices? See Figure 67 (note the exaggerated miter crown).[124] Fortunately nothing came of this conceit. A two-headed eagle has a certain dignity and symmetry, and a balanced symbolism can be imagined for it (see pages 88-89 below). But a three-headed eagle is just grotesque.[125]

As the double eagle came to stand for the Empire, the Empire came to stand for the German nation and indeed by extension the Christian (that is, Catholic) world. This identification was symbolized by a special form of the eagle called the *Quaternion-Adler*. In a Quaternion, the Emperor (and usually but not always the electors who chose him) stand at the top, and beneath him (or them), in groups of four, stand representatives of every other order in the Empire: four dukes, four counts, four knights, four cities, and so forth, down to four farmers.[126] Often these were human figures, each one holding his arms or the arms of his office.[127]

But in another kind of Quaternion, like that by Hans Burgkmair the Elder shown on the back cover of this book, the double eagle represents the Empire, with the crucified Jesus at its center. The groups of four (here tellingly called *members* [*Glieder*] of the Empire) are represented by their arms alone, spread out on the eagle's wings.[128] Burgkmair also created the remarkable image used as the frontispiece to this book (page 14), where a series of figures adorn the eagle's body – the emperor with embodiments of state and church, the seven liberal arts, the nine muses, and the judgment of Paris. On its wings are

---

[123]   *Das Wappenbuch Conrads von Grünenberg*, note 59, frame 0009; see also frame 0007.

[124]   I am grateful to Professor Hanns Hohmann of San Jose State University in California for help in reading the archaic German script in Grünenberg's painting.

[125]   Also of course the emperor, when he had actually *become* emperor, usually was also King of the Romans anyway, and so a three-headed version would not have served much purpose.

[126]   There were usually ten such groups, adding up to 40, a special number that appeared often in the Bible. The farmers were represented by cities or other corporations, or magnates, not by actual farmers.

[127]   The *Schedelsche Weltchronik*, by Hartmann Schedel (Augsburg, 1483) is an excellent example of this kind of Quaternion. It can be seen on Wikimedia Commons at tinyurl.com/mpt8pjk, with annotations that reveal the name of every order and example as the cursor mouses over it.

[128]   Note also the firesteels in the corners, striking fire with their flints against stones. These are a badge of the Order of the Golden Fleece, which passed to the Habsburg Dynasty by the Burgundian Inheritance, see pages 45-46 below.

medallions representing the seven days of creation and the seven mechanical arts. These figures are an epitome of the civilization of Burgkmair's time, and that he projected them all onto the double eagle shows how the Empire was considered the matrix and armature of that civilization.[129]

Sigismund was the last Emperor of the Luxemburg dynasty. He was succeeded in 1440 as King of the Romans by Frederick III, who became the first Habsburg Emperor in 1452.[130] As a practical (although not a legal) matter the Empire remained hereditary in the Habsburg family until it was dissolved in 1806.

THE DOUBLE EAGLE IN SPAIN AND THE NETHERLANDS

SPAIN

Frederick III, who consolidated the Habsburg family's dynastic rule in Austria, died in 1493. He was succeeded by his son Maximilian, with whom he had reigned jointly for ten years. Maximilian, who became emperor in 1508,[131] had added hugely to the Habsburg dominions by his brilliant marriage to Mary the Rich, heiress of Burgundy, in 1477. With her came the so-called Burgundian Inheritance comprising most of the Low Countries as well as other territories.[132] Their son Philip (called *Schöne*, the Handsome) inherited these

---

[129] The woodcut in the frontsipiece was created to honor Conrad Celtes (1459-1508), a German humanist and poet, who founded a college for poets in Vienna (the *Collegium Poetarum* in the title of Burgkmair's image). The wreaths in the eagle's beaks allude to his appointment as poet laureate by Emperor Frederick III, and later honors given to him by Maximilian I. Note by the eagle's left talon (as seen by the viewer) a shield with a single-headed eagle, with the arms of Austria-Burgundy on a breastshield; by the other talon are the arms of Austria alone.

[130] Rudolf of Habsburg was King of the Romans from 1273 to 1291, but was never emperor. There was one brief break in Habsburg occupation of the imperial office after Sigismund, when Maria Theresa came to the Austrian throne in 1740. See note 153 below. But by 1745 it was safely Habsburg-controlled again, in the person of her husband, Emperor Franz I.

[131] By special permission of Pope Julius II, he was allowed to assume the title *emperor-elect* without a papal coronation.

[132] Some of the territories in the Low Countries were imperial fiefs (held from the Empire by feudal tenure) and others were not. But even those parts which had been imperial fiefs were not Habsburg dominions before the Burgundian Marriage. Meanwhile Bohemia, Hungary and Croatia passed under Habsburg rule when King Louis II Jagiełłon, husband of an Austrian princess, died childless in the aftermath of the Battle of Mohács in 1526.

The Burgundian Marriage was celebrated by a spectacular procession, depicted in a work called the *Triumphzug Kaiser Maximilians I* [Triumphal procession of Emperor Maximilian I]. It was illustrated by a vast collection of woodcuts 177 feet (54 meters) long, including works by Hans Burgkmair, Albrecht Dürer, and others, with much heraldic detail. The *Triumphzug* can be seen

(footnote continues →)

lands, at the age of three, when Mary died in 1482. His father Maximilian I served as regent until 1494, when at 16 Philip began active rule of the Burgundian lands. Two years later, in 1496, Philip married Joanna of Castile; he became King of Castile in 1506, but died the same year at the age of 26. By a series of unexpected deaths and dynastic events, Charles, the son of Joanna and Philip, inherited not only Burgundy but all the elements of what became the Spanish Kingdom: Castile, Leon, Aragon, Navarre and Granada.[133] When Emperor Maximilian died in 1519, Charles succeeded him as German king and King of the Romans (he became emperor in 1530). Frederick, Maximilian and Charles all followed the traditional practice of using only a single-headed eagle on their seals as Kings of the Romans, not assuming the double eagle until they became emperors.

So by marriages and inheritances Charles (left; the First of Spain, but known in history as Emperor Charles V), without even trying much, concentrated in his hands a wider empire than had been seen in Europe since Charlemagne, *plus* the new Spanish colonial empire in the Americas and elsewhere, far greater than the old Empire, greater indeed than Europe itself.[134] Figure 68 is a Spanish coin of Charles V, issued after he became Emperor. His arms, carried on a breastshield by the double eagle, reflected this expanse of power.

Figure 69 shows these arms, in a typical arrangement (they were not always the same), on the licensing page of a book published in 1536.[135] The first quarter contains fields for the Spanish territories: León (lion), Castile (castle), Aragon (vertical stripes), Granada (pomegranate) and Navarre (chain), as well as Jerusalem (cross), Hungary (horizontal

---

(footnote continues …)

digitally on the University of Graz website at tinyurl.com/kkxfxbz, and has been reprinted (as *Triumphal Procession of Maximilian I*) as a Dover book (New York, 1964).

[133] Castile, Leon and Galicia had been united by earlier dynastic marriages and inheritances. Charles' rule in the Spanish territories was in right of his mother Joanna, who was confined as insane (perhaps unjustly) for most of her life. She remained *nominally* Queen of Castile and Leon, and later Aragon too, until her death in 1555. There was a saying about the Habsburgs, back when saying were in Latin: *Bella gerant alii; tu, felix Austria, nubes* [let others wage wars; you, happy Austria, marry].

[134] Spain also claimed the Philippines (by Magellan's "discovery" in 1521), and established an official government there in 1565. Other lands outside the Americas were eventually added to the Spanish colonial empire, which did not terminate completely until 1969, and still (2014) retains the Canary Islands and exclaves in Morocco..

[135] The imperial license allowed the book to be published.

stripes) and Sicily (stripes of Aragon with a black eagle). The second quarter has fields for Austria (horizontal stripe), "Old Burgundy" (diagonal stripes), Burgundy-Valois (fleurs-de-lys and checked border), Brabant (light-colored lion), Flanders (black lion) and Tyrol (eagle).[136]

Figure 70 shows a version of the imperial arms on the dedication page of a history of the conquest of Peru. The eagle stands on an idealized scene of South America.[137] Figure 71, from a booklet published in 1550, has a simpler arrangement, the shield showing just Austria and Burgundy. This was often used, on coins and elsewhere, where size or graphic need or preference required less detail. Note the pillars and the motto *Plus Oultre* [more beyond], added to the imperial arms by Charles V.[138] Figure 72, from around 1547,

---

[136]   The arrangement and rendition of the fields is rough and in some places not entirely accurate. Observe, though, how all eight castles of Castile line up diagonally from top left to bottom right.

I note parenthetically that the different fields on these arms provide a gallery of the types of early heraldry. There are geometrical forms – horizontal stripes for Hungary and Austria, vertical stripes for Aragon and Sicily, diagonal stripes for Old Burgundy, and the checked (*compony*) border of Burgundy-Valois. There are the archetypal solar animals – three lions (León, Flanders and Brabant) and two eagles (Sicily and Tyrol). There is one artifact (the castle of Castile) – two if you count the cross of Jerusalem. Three of the fields have elements developed from the metal reinforcements of pre-heraldic shields – the borders on the two Burgundian fields, and the chain of Navarre, which in its earliest form was a radial reinforcement called an *escarbuncle* (see Ignacio Vicente Cascante, *Heraldica General y Fuentes de las Armas de España* [General heraldry and sources of the arms of Spain] (Barcelona, 1956), 437-449, and especially the proto-heraldic seal of Sancho VII at 443, fig. 276). The fleurs-de-lys of Burgundy-Valois were not really lilies, but stylizations of the archetypal bud, a symbol of regeneration (see for example its early use on scepters on pre-heraldic French seals in William M. Hinkle, *The Fleurs de Lis of the Kings of France 1285-1488* (Carbondale [Illinois], 1991), plates 3-4). The castle of Castile, the lion (Latin *leo*) of León (from Latin *legio*, meaning *legion*), and the pomegranate of Granada (Spanish *granada*) are *canting charges* (that is, puns), a common feature of early heraldry.

[137]   The motto around the South American scene reads IN OMNEM TERRAM EXIVIT SONUS EORUM. This quotation from Psalm 18:5 (Psalm 19 in the Catholic Bible), reads in English *their voice goes out into all the earth*. Poetically we may imagine that the plural subject *their* refers to the two heads of the eagle, and *their voice* the eagle's call.

[138]   The pillars represent the so-called Pillars of Hercules – Gibraltar and a corresponding mount on the African side of the Strait that forms the western boundary of the Mediterranean Sea. Opinion is divided as to just which African mountain is the other pillar. The old saying *nec plus ultra* [no more beyond] was changed to include the newly discovered Western Hemisphere beyond Gibraltar, much of which as noted was part of Charles' newest empire. The pillars and the motto are part of the Spanish national arms to this day. They were sometimes shown with one royal and one imperial crown.

has the double eagle arms more elegantly rendered in a woodcut by Heinrich Vogtherr the Elder.[139]

Such an enormous empire was too much for Charles V – maybe it would have been too much for anyone. In 1555 he abdicated all his territories and titles[140] and retired to a monastery. He directed that his empire be divided – Spain, and the Netherlands (soon to be lost to revolution), and territories in Italy, and America, to go to his son Philip, who would become King Philip II of Spain, and the other Habsburg lands, including Austria (with its claims to Bohemia, Hungary and other territories), *and* the imperial title, to his brother, who would become Emperor Ferdinand I when Charles died in 1558.[141] From this time on the imperial title, and the double eagle, were identified with Habsburg Austria and its tributary lands, as the power of the so-called Holy Roman Empire, its political relevance already in decline, shrank to insignificance except as an ornament of the House of Habsburg.

Spain was not part of the Holy Roman Empire, and with the transfer of the Empire to the Austrian branch of the Habsburgs the double eagle passed out of general use in Spain and its colonies. A few relics remain. Philip I and Charles V "prodigally" granted towns and noble families the right to use the double eagle.[142] For example, the double eagle supporting the Spanish arms was granted by imperial concession to the city of Toledo in Spain and to the city of Tunja in what is now the Department of Boyacá, Colombia. Figure 73 shows the arms of Toledo on the city gate. Figure 74, from a monument in Mexico, combines the double eagle with the Aztec eagle-and-snake motif.[143] Figure 75, the arms of the Academia Boyacense de Historia established in Tunja in 1905, is an example of the continuing vitality of the double eagle image long after the empire it stood for had vanished.

---

[139]   Note the elaboration of the miter-crown. The motto *Plus Ultra* is here given in old German (*Noch Weytter*).

[140]   Except for the County of Charolais in France – maybe he thought it best to keep *something*, because you never know.

[141]   The Imperial Diet [*Reichstag*] did not ratify Charles' abdication, so the imperial throne did not become vacant until he died. Philip II of Spain was the husband of Queen Mary I (Tudor) of England, and so had pretensions to be king of England through the principle of the *crown matrimonial*; this idea made little progress in England, and anyway Mary died in 1558.

[142]   *Pródigamente*, said Vicente Cascante, note 136 above, 179.

[143]   See also Figure 213 for an example from Bolivia. The eagle-and-snake is an archetypal image found in many cultures ancient and modern, and stands for the ascendancy of heaven over earth, good over evil, light over darkness, and many similar dichotomies.

Despite the eclipse of the double eagle in the Spanish Empire after the abdication of Charles V, some writers continued to use it in political and theological works defending and glorifying the Spanish monarchy.[144] A notable example is Juan de Caramuel y Lobkowitz, *Declaración Mystica de las Armas de España, Invictamente Belicosas* [Mystical declaration of the arms of Spain, invincibly warlike] (Brussels, 1636), an "extreme defense of the preeminence of the Spanish monarchy over all others and of its rights to territories."[145] A remarkable illustration from this work appears in Figure 76 – the eagle has the legs of a bull and four wings, its body covered with eyes.[146]

NETHERLANDS

Although parts of the Netherlands were not within the Empire, other parts were, and most of them were included in the Burgundian Inheritance. The Protestant northern provinces broke away from Spanish domination after a long and unpleasant war, declaring an independent republic in 1581. But the Catholic provinces remained under Hapsburg control – first Spanish, later Austrian – until conquered by France in 1794.[147] Figure 77 is a flag used there during the later Austrian period.

---

[144] I am grateful to Steven Thiry and Professor Luc Duerloo of the University of Antwerp for making me aware of this literature in their paper "The Eagle Resurrected: The Abdication of Emperor Charles V, the Spanish Monarchy and the Reinvention of the Imperial Eagle," delivered at the XXXI International Congress of Genealogical and Heraldic Sciences in Oslo in August 2014. It is to be published in the forthcoming Proceedings of the Congress.

[145] Inmaculada Rodríguez and Víctor Mínguez, "Symbolical Explanation of the Spanish Coats of Arms According to Juan de Caramuel (1636)," *Emblematica*, 16:223-251 (New York, 2008), 225-6. This thorough illustrated article is available digitally through academica.edu at tinyurl.com/qduzey4. See also Víctor Mínguez, "Juan de Caramuel y su Declaración Mystica de las Armas de España" [Juan de Caramuel and his mystical declaration of the arms of Spain], *Archivo Español de Arte* [Spanish art archive] (Madrid, 2007), 80:395-410, available digitally at tinyurl.com/pflngdp.

[146] The eyes and the extra wings echo, without quite reproducing, the vision of cherubim reported by the prophet Ezekiel ("And their whole body … and their wings … were full of eyes …" [Ezekiel 10:12]). Caramuel's treatise, while a monument of abstract and poetical reasoning, is worthless as genuine heraldic commentary. He says, for example, that the lion and castle, in truth merely plays on the names of Léon and Castile, were the emblems of Spain "before Hercules" and really symbolize occult truths about the Spanish kings and the Catholic religion. Rodriguez and Mínguez, note 145 above, 233-37.

[147] First called the Spanish Netherlands, there was an attempt in 1599 to set up a separate Habsburg Netherlands under a Habsburg archduke. They reverted to Spanish rule in 1621 when the archduke died without children. In 1714 the Habsburgs lost control of Spain when the War of the Spanish Succession ended badly for them, and the Catholic Netherlands, along with provinces in Italy, were transferred to Austrian control. They did not become an independent country until the creation of Belgium in 1830.

The double eagle passed into wide use in Flanders and nearby lands after the 13th century coinage of Marguerite of Constantinople,[148] and it appeared frequently in Netherlands heraldry. Figure 78 is a seal of a Dutch nobleman, Engelbert Ludick van Dijck, from 1318 (before the double eagle became an imperial emblem); Figure 79 is woodcut of the arms of the Margraves of Antwerp, with a chief of the Empire, from a book published in 1500; Figure 80 shows the arms of Jean-Louis d'Elderen, Prince-Bishop of Liège, with a double eagle supporter. The double eagle figures in the arms of at least 25 Dutch cities and towns.[149] Figure 81 is the modern flag of the City of Arnhem, whose arms are a blue double eagle on white.

THE DOUBLE EAGLE IN AUSTRIA

As noted, after the division of the Hapsburg lands by Charles V, the imperial office fell to the Austrian branch. From 1558, the Empire was centered on Austria, and on the Austrian-controlled lands which increased as Turkish hegemony receded in the Balkans, and on Italian lands transferred to the Austrian branch after the extinction of the Habsburg line in Spain in 1714. The old practice continued, for a while, of using a one headed eagle for the King of the Romans, and two heads when he acceded to the imperial title. For example the sumptuous seals of Ferdinand I from before and after his imperial accession are nearly identical except for the inscription and the number of heads.[150]

Although the Empire was now Austrian, or at least Habsburg, in theory the Emperor was still the overlord of Germany (and indeed German-speaking Austria was then considered a leading part of Germany). But the Reformation, and its new principle that the prince had the right to determine the religion of his state, split the old Catholic Europe and the political coherence of the old Catholic Empire.[151] The Thirty Years War (1618-48) devastated Germany, and in the settlements that followed the feudal basis of imperial

---

[148]   See pages 41-42 above; and see Soloviev (1935), note 6, 141.

[149]   Including some whose arms are displayed with an imperial crown (*keizerskroon*), for example Bolsward, Nijmegen and Tiel. The double eagle of Groningen has already been mentioned – see page 37. For a list of Dutch double-eagle towns, see Klaes Sierskma, *De Gemeentewapens van Nederland* [Arms of Dutch communities] (Utrecht, 1968), 252.

[150]   In Posse, note 84, compare seals at vol. 3, plate 21, no.1 and plate 22, no. 4. Maximilian II did the same – compare seals in Posse, vol. 3, plates 29 and 30. After Charles V there was rarely any significant interval between assumption of the two titles, except where (as with Ferdinand I and Joseph I) the title of King of the Romans had been assumed during the preceding imperial reign.

[151]   This principle was called by the Latin phrase *cuius regio, eius religio*, meaning roughly *whose territory, his religion*.

paramountcy was fatally undermined. The Peace of Westphalia that ended the war moved the European state system finally and definitively from a feudal to a nation-state basis.[152]

This new conception of the state finally ended *practical* imperial pretensions in Germany (apart from Austria). The *theoretical* structure of the old Empire remained, but it was now largely irrelevant to political and international reality. As the Empire grew less powerful, the Habsburg enterprise based on Austria (but including states such as Bohemia, Hungary and others) grew more powerful, until finally the new structure absorbed what was left of the old.

Beginning with the concentration of crowns under Charles V, the emperors developed the eagle's breastshield as a kind of billboard of their sovereignties. But their sovereignties were so numerous and complicated that the breastshield, before usually limited to one or two fields (usually Austria and Burgundy), began to overwhelm the eagle. We have seen this already in a coin of Charles V (Figure 68). At the very start of the Austrian period in 1558, on a coronation medal of Ferdinand I (1558) (Figure 85), the breastshield is so complex that it is quite illegible and almost completely obscures the eagle that is supposed to bear it.

The *genealogical arms* of Austria, adopted after the marriage of Maria Theresa (left) to Joseph of Lorraine in 1740, added Lorraine to the heartshield.[153] Where it had been divided in half vertically (*parti per pale*) between Austria and Burgundy (see Figure 71), now it was divided vertically three ways (*tierced in pale*): the Habsburg lion, the horizontal stripe (*fess*) of Austria, and the diagonal stripe (*bend*) of Lorraine.[154] This three-way

---

[152]   It also recognized the independence of Switzerland from the Empire.

[153]   For constitutional reasons Maria Theresa, as a woman, could not be emperor, but by the Pragmatic Sanction of 1713 she *could* inherit the Austrian lands, and after a brief hiatus her husband Duke Francis of Lorraine became emperor in her place. His eagle had a breastshield of Lorraine and Tuscany (arms of Medici), a territory he inherited; hers had Hungary, Habsburg and a heartshield of Austria.

[154]   On the bend of Lorraine were three curious figures called *alerions* – birds without beaks or feet. Despite fanciful stories, such as that they commemorated a lucky shot by an early Duke of Lorraine who killed three birds with one arrow, in truth the alerions were simply a *canting charge* (a pun) and an anagram – *alerion* for *Lorraine*.

There have been many other variations. For example, a seal of Rudolf II showed Austria and Castile on the heartshield, reflecting the pact under which the Austrian and Spanish branches would succeed to the lands of the other in case of extinction of the line. The Spanish line failed in 1700, but when the Hapsburgs lost the War of the Spanish Succession that followed, the throne of Spain went to the Bourbons instead. Rudolf II's seal for Hungary showed Austria and Hungary on the heartshield.

division remained in official use until the end of the Austrian monarchy in 1918, and is still used by the Habsburg family.[155] Figure 82 is the definitive version of the *small arms* of the Empire (1848 pattern), by the master Austrian heraldic artist Hugo Gerard Ströhl.[156] Figure 83 is an elaboration of the genealogical arms, from an 1880 heraldic pattern book by Emil Doepler the Younger. Austrian coins often bore just the plain fess of Austria on the breastshield.

The nominal, theoretical, shadowy and almost fictional Empire survived until 1806, when it was formally dissolved by Emperor Francis II. Napoleon, already Emperor of the French, had defeated him (and the Russians) at the Battle of Austerlitz the previous year and was reorganizing the state structure of Germany and northern Italy at his whim. Joseph feared Napoleon would make himself Holy Roman Emperor, and disbanded the Empire to avoid this. He had taken the precaution shortly before, in 1804, of creating a second, backup Empire of Austria, consisting of the Habsburg possessions, with himself as Emperor Francis I (rather than II as before). This had the dual function of uniting these possessions into a somewhat more coherent political structure and ensuring the continued imperial status of the Habsburg dynasty. The new empire also continued the double eagle as a state and imperial emblem – only a close examination of the heraldic details, and the Latin inscriptions on the coins and seals, shows the difference.

Even the Austrian small arms included the Order of the Golden Fleece on a jeweled collar around the shield.[157] Other attributes were added to the middle and great arms.[158] On a seal of Leopold I from 1696, for example (Figure 86), the eagle carries both sword and scepter, and the collar of the Golden Fleece, and the nimbus, *and* baroque architectural details around the shield, *and* a coronet around its throat, *and* a revised

---

[155]   For example at the Vienna funeral of Otto von Habsburg, head of the House, in 2011.

[156]   The arms in Figure 82, created as a line drawing, are hatched with a conventional pattern of fine lines and stippling to indicate the colors. This convention – vertical for red, horizontal for blue, stippled for yellow, etc. – is called the *Petra Sancta system*.

    Austria, like other sovereignties with complicated heraldry, had state arms in three levels of complexity: *small, middle and great arms*. Austria largely abandoned its great arms after the constitutional changes of 1867, reflecting the elevation of Hungary to a co-realm with Austria and the definitive loss of the Italian possessions.

[157]   This prestigious Catholic order was founded by Philip III (the Good), Duke of Burgundy, in 1430, and was part of the Burgundian Inheritance. The Order still survives, in Spanish and Austrian branches.

[158]   These are described in detail in Franz Gall, *Österreichische Wappenkunde* [Austrian heraldry] (Vienna, 1966). For a superb treatment of the heraldic background and changes, beautifully illustrated, see Hugo Gerard Ströhl, *Oesterreichisch-Ungarische Wappenrolle* [Austro-Hungarian armorial] (Vienna, 1900; modern reprint Schleinbach [Austria], 2010).

imperial crown reflecting the actual new imperial crown made for Rudolf II in 1602, *plus* arms of the crown lands around the border.[159] Emperor Francis I (reigned 1745-65) sometimes substituted for this ponderous structure the genealogical arms (or just his cypher) on the cross insignia of the Grand Master of the Teutonic Order (*Hoch- und Deutschmeister*) – this office too was now hereditary in the Habsburg dynasty.[160] See Figure 87.

As noted the genealogical arms, with only three fields, were among the simplest arms on the breast of the double eagle. Other, more complex heraldic arrangements were in frequent use on coins and elsewhere, adding quarterings for Bohemia, Hungary (including eventually a second crown), other lands to the south and east such as Tyrol and Transylvania, and territories in Italy, such as Tuscany, Parma and Milan (for which the arms of the Medici, Farnese and Visconti, their former rulers, were incongruously borne). Quarterings for territories long lost or extinguished, such as the Crusader Kingdom of Jerusalem, were not removed from the most complex renderings, lest this be taken as abandonment of a territorial claim.[161] Figure 84 (the "full" Austrian arms, not used in practice after 1866) is an elaborate instance.[162] Sometimes one (or only a few) of these territorial arms was used alone – Figure 88, a 1777 Transylvanian gold ducat of Maria Theresa, is a beautiful example. There are dozens of variations.

In Figure 90 we see the reverse of one of the most important coins of the period, the Maria Theresa thaler, with a manageable number of quarterings. So popular was this coin for its reliable silver content that it continues to be minted (2014) for use as a *trade dollar*, being in high demand for example in East Africa. After 1780 even the date did not

---

[159]   The crown, a masterpiece of gold work, enamel and jewels, may be seen in the *Weltliche Schatzkammer* [secular treasury] at the Hofburg in Vienna. For a description, with pictures, see the Wikipedia article at tinyurl.com/d9x7wfd. For a fuller discussion, see Edward Twining [Lord Twining], *A History of the Crown Jewels of Europe* (London, 1960), 7-10. For a thorough treatment with pictures, but in German, see e.g. Hermann Fillitz, *Die Österreichische Kaiserkrone* [The Austrian imperial crown] (Vienna, 1959).

[160]   In former times this once powerful knightly chivalric order had exercised sovereignty in parts of northeastern Europe. A *cypher*, meaning a (usually) royal monogram, is different from a *cipher*, meaning either a code or the number zero.

[161]   This practice led to a cluttering of dynastic arms in other countries as well. England included a quartering for France until 1801. The great arms of the Savoyard Kings of Piedmont, forerunners to the Kings of Italy, included quarterings for Saxony and Hanover, representing the supposed overlordship of Widukind, a semi-legendary eighth-century warlord – they also quartered Jerusalem, and Cyprus too.

[162]   For a detailed blazon of the Austrian *écu-complet* [complete shield], in English, with all quarterings identified, see Woodward, note 74, 494-504.

change.[163] Many imperial and archducal seals surrounded the eagle with arms of subordinate territories, and there had been specifically Austrian Quaternion eagles.[164] But not until 1806 do we see the first appearance of the Austrian imperial eagle with the arms of the crown lands on its wings.[165] In slightly varying forms, this was the principal emblem of authority (*Hoheitszeichen*) in the Austrian lands until the end of the Empire in 1918. The classic 1867 version of these *middle arms* (by Ströhl) appears on the inside front cover of this book.[166]

The final development of the Austrian imperial eagle took place during the long reign of Emperor Francis Joseph I (right), known in history as Franz Josef, who came to the throne in the busy revolutionary year 1848 and stayed there until 1916, halfway through World War I.[167] In 1867 a basic constitutional change created the Dual Monarchy of Austria and Hungary, familiarly called Austria-Hungary or the Austro-Hungarian Empire. This change was reflected in the arms. There were some later heraldic changes, too, of interest mainly to specialists, with additions to or rearrangement of territories in the Balkans. In some cases, such as the so-called Kingdom of Illyria, no authentic arms existed and new ones had to be created. In 1915, just as Austria was about to lose World War I and its empire and monarchy, and the whole of the *ancien régime* was about to disappear all over Europe, a final elaborate *combined* version of the arms was issued. Austria and Hungary were shown in equal size, with the genealogical arms in

---

[163] Except by adding an X, as in this modern example. Foreign mints also struck the Maria Theresa trade dollar – the British continued to mint them until 1962. The portrait of the empress on page 51 is the obverse of the same coin.

[164] An Austrian and also a Spanish Habsburg *Quaternionadler* may be seen at Figures 7a and 8a on the Héraldique et Manuscrits [Heraldry and manuscripts] page of the Encre et Lumière [Ink and Illumination] forum website, at tinyurl.com/log37jz. This page is a rich source of heraldic images, both Habsburg and others. For a drawing by Franz Gall of the double eagle with the arms of the *electors* on its wings, based on an example from 1690, see Gall, note 158, plate 2.

[165] For an image, see *id.*, plate 11, facing p. 63.

[166] Counter-clockwise from upper left, on the 1867 version: Hungary, Galicia, Lower Austria, Salzburg, Styria, Tyrol, Carinthia, Moravia/Silesia, Transylvania, Illyria, Bohemia. Note that the crowns on these small shields differ in detail, reflecting the constitutional history and position of each territory.

[167] He reigned 68 years, until the age of 86. In later years he was known as the Old Gentleman (*der alte Herr*).

the middle, supported by the griffins of the Habsburg dynasty. See Figure 89. As was so often the case, the finest flower of this nation's heraldic art did not appear until the end.

The Empire still had a military force when the Austrian period began – indeed it had two. The Army of the Empire (*Reichsheer*) was a standing army subject to the Imperial Diet, or Parliament (*Reichstag*), levied on a territorial basis from the Imperial circles (*Reichskreise*) in contingents of predetermined strength. The Army of the Emperor (*Kaiserliche Armee*) was raised by the Habsburg emperor from all over the Empire (with some territories excluded).[168]

This is not the place to develop the constitutional or military history of the late Empire. I mention it because some imperial military colours (that is, regimental or unit flags) bore the double eagle. It was not the only pattern for this period – many colours bore the initials of the colonel, or an imperial cypher, a regional or dynastic coat of arms, a religious image, or some other design. But there were dozens of vivid variations on the double eagle motif. Figures 91-94 are colours of regiments in the Imperial Army during the 18th century. The first of these is a standard pattern regimental colour for a cuirassier regiment, with the arms of the colonel painted or embroidered on the back.[169] The second is the reverse of a Hungarian heiduck regimental colour; note the Madonna and child on the breastshield.[170] The others are from German and Netherlands Catholic regiments. Also included (Figure 95) is the colour of the Schützenkompanie Tramin, a local Tyrolean rifle militia; its colorful flag (a modern reproduction of an example from 1779) is typical of the genre.

Double-eagle military flags of this period often bore the Austrian two-part breastshield

---

168   For example, the *Kaiserlicher Armee* could not be recruited in the territories of the electoral princes. There were also other divisions of the Imperial/Austrian military establishment. Wikipedia (at tinyurl.com/kyj4dc7) gives this handy list for the major wars of the Imperial Army, which shows the Empire pretty constantly engaged: Long War (1593-1606), Thirty Years' War (1618-1648), Second Northern War (1655-1660), Austro-Turkish War (1663-1664), Scanian War (1674-1679), Nine Years' War (1688-1697), Great Turkish War (1683-1699), War of the Spanish Succession (1701-1714), Second Austro-Turkish War (1714-1718), War of the Polish Succession (1732-1738), Austro-Russian-Turkish War (1736-1739). In many of these wars (but not the Thirty Years War) both imperial armies worked together.

169   Cuirassiers were mounted cavalry with firearms.

170   Heiducks, originally irregular brigands, were formed into regular infantry regiments under Habsburg command for use on the Hungarian borders and elsewhere.

    "[T]he Imperial double-eagle always carried the sword in its right hand claw and the scepter in its left hand claw. Eagles carrying the orb in the right and sword/scepter in the left are flags of the Imperial circles." Robert Hall and Giancarlo Boeri, *Uniforms and Flags of the Imperial Austrian Army* 1683-1720 (n.p., 2008) (CD), 134.

(Austria and Burgundy). Imperial and Austrian symbolism tended to merge as the *Reichsheer* was under Austrian control. Figure 96 is the 1754 version of the standard Austrian/imperial infantry colour.[171] The zig-zag border, called a *Zackenrand*, was a distinctively Austrian ornament. Hungary did have a short coastline on the Adriatic – in Figure 97 we see a rendering of an Austro-Hungarian naval ensign, circa 1716, by Željko Heimer.[172]

There were double eagle survivals in Germany even after the end of the old Empire. From 1848 to 1852 the German Confederation (*Deutscher Bund*, a precursor to the unified Germany of later years) flew a set of flags featuring the imperial double eagle (Figure 98 is its war flag).[173] When the second German Empire was organized in 1871, the Principality of Schwarzburg was one of its constituent states.[174] Schwarzburg kept its arms, with the imperial double eagle, until the end of the Second Empire in 1918. Figure 99 shows the arms of Schwarzburg-Rudolstadt – the fork and comb in the base are the emblems of the prince's office as *Reichserbstallmeister* [Hereditary imperial stable-master].[175] Some of the imperial cities like Lübeck and Cologne continue to use the double eagle as a supporter for their civic arms – Figure 62 is a modern example.

The Austrian double eagle served many official purposes – on coins, on stamps, on arms patents and imperial decrees, on military and chivalric orders and decorations of chivalry,

---

[171] This flag had slightly different designs on its two sides. In the illustration the *hoist*, where the pole attached. is shown at the right – the letters FC IM stand for *Franciscus Coregens Imperator* [Francis, Joint Ruler, Emperor], and MT on the back for Maria Theresa. Other cyphers were used in other reigns.

[172] "It is hardly possible," writes Heimer about the Austrian navy, "to claim that there existed a unique design of the flag that would be carried on all imperial ships. The obtaining of the flag was a duty of each captain and he would order and buy flags of a design of his pleasure and the skill of the manufacturer within the general outline – golden and black flags with the black double-headed eagle. This was enough to identify the ship as being under Habsburg rule. The various designs found in literature include a golden-black bicolour with the eagle in canton, golden flags with multiple black stripes with or without the eagle in the centre or in the canton, and so on." From the Flags of the World website at tinyurl.com/lw99rgq (citation omitted).

[173] The eagle appears only in the canton, but the basic colors black-red-gold, the colors of the modern German flag, have their origin in the arms of the Empire: on a gold field, a black eagle with red tongue, beak, and legs (*or, a double eagle sable, langued, beaked and membered gules*). See discussion on the German Confederation page of the Flags of the World website at tinyurl.com/kuxejpw.

[174] Actually *two* of its constituent states – Schwarzburg-Rudolstadt and Schwarzburg-Sondershausen.

[175] The double eagle also appeared on the standards of both princes. For beautiful color images see Hugo Gerard Ströhl, *Deutsche Wappenrolle* [German armorial] (Stuttgart, 1897), plate 20, nos. 23, 26.

on military uniforms and buttons and epaulets and belt buckles, and elsewhere. Figure 100 shows an Austrian army belt buckle from the period 1867-1915; Figure 101 is the badge of the Austrian Order of the Iron Crown.[176] The double eagle was the main charge in a series of flags denoting rank – Figure 103 is the 1894 pattern of the imperial standard. It was also the basic charge on the Empire's military flags – indeed the phrase *unter dem Doppeladler* [under the double eagle] was Austrian slang for *in military service* (see Figure 104).

In Austria, one of the centers of the art nouveau and art deco movements, it was natural in the last years of the Empire to find double eagles in both styles. Figure 105 is an art nouveau example, from a military label (*Militärmark*) of the 11th Dragoon Regiment.[177] Figure 106 is an art deco design by Koloman Moser.[178] Figure 107 is the emblem of the Austrian Red Cross under the Empire.

Three images form a coda to the Austrian double eagle. In 1934 a fascist government came to power in republican Austria, which ruled what it called the Federal State of Austria (*Bundesstaat Österreich*) until its absorption into Hitler's Germany in 1938. This ephemeral regime used the double eagle on its flag and state symbols. Figure 108 is its rank flag for high officials, adopted in 1936; Figure 109 is the emblem of Vienna used in the same period.[179]

---

[176] The Austrian Order of the Iron Crown was founded by Emperor Francis I in 1815, as an order of chivalry for Italy (and for services related to the Empire's Italian possessions). It supplanted Napoleon's order of the same name, and was abolished at the end of the Empire in 1918. The eagle is shown standing on the Iron Crown of Lombardy, an early medieval object used in the coronation ritual of the Kings of Italy until the 19th century. It was part of the Hapsburg regalia until 1866, when the Austrians, having lost the Third Italian War of Independence, surrendered the crown to the new Italian government. It appears above the shield in the arms of the Habsburg Kingdom of Lombardy-Venetia (Figure 102). For more on the Iron Crown, see Twining, note 159, 415-31. A color photograph of the Iron Crown appears on Wikimedia Commons at tinyurl.com/k5x6aq9.

[177] *Militärmarken* were unofficial labels issued privately by regiments and other military organizations in many countries of Europe, for fund-raising, morale and propaganda purposes.

[178] Koloman Moser (1868-1918) was one of the leading artists in the Vienna modernist style. He was a founding member of the Secession Movement and of the Wiener Werkstätt, and designed some Austrian postage stamps in the new styles. For more information on Moser, in English, see an unsigned August 14, 2013 article "Koloman Moser" in the Swiss on-line *Cosmopolis* magazine at tinyurl.com/l65zc3b.

[179] In 1925 the Vienna City Council declared the cross heartshield alone to be the arms of Vienna, but allowed an unofficial single-headed eagle supporter. When the Fascist regime restored the second head in 1934, they added a version of Charlemagne's crown. The 1925 arrangement was revived in 1945. See Peter Diem, "Die Symbole Wiens" (note 97), and "Civic Heraldry of

(footnote continues →)

Finally, the Adriatic port of Fiume (now Rijeka), Austrian from the 15th century and site of the Austrian imperial naval academy, had a coat of arms with a relatively naturalistic double eagle holding a jar from which water flowed into the sea (*fiume* is Italian for *river*). See Figure 110. A version of these arms is still used by Rijeka in the modern Croatian republic.[180]

The Double Eagle in Italy

Overlordship in Italy made some sense for Charlemagne, and for the Pope too in that period. But when the Empire was revived in the 10th century as an essentially German enterprise, it made less sense. It required constant warfare, and indeed subduing Italy became the expensive, wasteful and distracting obsession of the German kings. This is not the place to recount those nearly endless efforts. It is sufficient to say that by the time Sigismund adopted the double eagle as an emblem of the Empire in the early 15th century, imperial control of Italy was largely a thing of the past. The rise of the Italian city-republics, and their eventual transformation under successor tyrannies into substantial states, made imperial overlordship even more of a fiction than it had been before. By this time imperial intervention in Italy was mainly aimed against the invading French, another story this is not the place to tell. As a souvenir of those times, see  at right the evocative image of Maximilian Sforza, deposed Duke of Milan, appealing to Emperor Maximilian for military help around 1513.[181]

(*footnote continues ...*)

Austria" on the Heraldry of the World website at tinyurl.com/o4n9kpj.

[180]   Thanks to Željko Heimer for noticing that in these arms, very unusually, both heads face in the same direction.

[181]   *The Restoration of Milan to the Empire*, by Albrecht Altdorfer the Elder (around 1514). Maximilian Sforza, Duke of Milan (left, with the serpent flag), pleads with Emperor Maximilian I (right, with the double eagle flag) for help in recovering his duchy from the French. Below are the arms of the prince-electors of the Empire. Left: Archbishops of Trier, Cologne, Mainz; right:

(*footnote continues* →)

58

Nevertheless the double eagle did leave some traces in Italy. The most interesting, because they still survive in significant numbers, are the black eagles on gold many Italian families place in the top field (the *chief*) of their shields, above their family arms. Figure 111 is the 16th century arms of Pope Alexander VIII (Ottoboni); there are other examples all over Italy. Sometimes the eagles have two heads, more often only one; the eagles may be crowned, or *ensigned* with crowns that float above their heads. This special chief, called a *capo dell'impero* (chief of the Empire) was sometimes granted to a family by the emperor as an augmentation.[182]

But the *capo dell'impero* was also sometimes assumed as a *chief of association* to indicate adherence to the imperial (or *Ghibelline*) party in the conflict between the emperor and the Pope, a factional division that later took on other forms and meanings.[183] The other side had a corresponding *capo d'angiò* (chief of Anjou) to indicate adherence to the opposing *Guelf* party.[184] In the *capo d'angiò* a red *label* separates with its pendent arms three gold fleurs-de-lys on a blue field.[185] See Figure 112 (Garganelli). There are even examples of both chiefs used at once.[186]

Sometimes the emperors granted important families a *quarto dell'impero*, meaning the right to *quarter* the arms of the Empire with their own – the Seregi di Cortesia of Venice,

---

(footnote continues ...)

Palatinate, Saxony, Brandenburg.

[182] The Malaspina of Venice have a *capo dell'impero* in red instead of gold.

[183] "Since the death of Conradin [the last heir of the Hohenstaufen emperors, in 1268], the discord of these factions was almost without object: it survived from habit and personal animosities, rather than from opposition of political interests." Pierre Daunou, *The Power of the Popes* (Paris, 1799). The quotation comes from chapter VI, but a page citation is not available as this work was consulted in an unpaginated (but word-searchable) electronic edition of the anonymous English translation (3d ed., 1838) of Daunou's *Essai historique sur la puissance temporelle des papes* [Historical essay on the temporal power of the Popes], found on Project Gutenberg at tinyurl.com/kcox9h8. Despite this irregular citation, it seems apt enough to quote anyway.

[184] Giovanni Santi-Mazzini, in his treatise *Araldica* [Heraldry] (Milan, 3d ed. 2007), 138, writes that the *capo dell'impero* was first granted as a concession by Emperor Frederick I (Barbarossa). But Barbarossa died in 1190, which seems too early for such a formal device.

[185] The arms of Anjou are the royal arms of France (three gold fleurs-de-lys on blue) within a red border. The *capo d'angiò* was originally awarded by Charles of Anjou (King Charles I of Naples, 1226-1285) to local adherents in his anti-imperial intervention in Italy. It seems likely, although I can't prove it, that the *capo dell'impero* was created in response to Charles' awards of the *capo d'angiò*.

[186] For example, the arms of the Salina of Romagna. See Sovereign Military Order of [St. John of] Jerusalem and Malta, *Elenco Storico della Nobilità Italiana* [Historical directory of the Italian nobility] (Rome, 1960), 463.

who were counts of the Holy Roman Empire, are an example.[187] See Figure 113. And some noble houses were given the right to place the imperial double eagle *behind* their arms, as a supporter. I have mentioned these augmentations, or *concessions* as they were sometimes called, in Spain and Spanish America. They were available in Spain during the relatively short reign of Charles V, the only emperor to rule there. But in Italy the emperors had much longer to make these concessions; and as they were intangible gifts from the emperor as the *fount of honor*, it did not matter for this purpose how much actual political power the emperor had in any particular place or moment.[188]

In later years, after the question of imperial pretensions in Italy had long been settled, Habsburg princes succeeded indigenous dynasties over much of Italy by military, diplomatic and matrimonial means, and by outright swaps of territory. Hapsburgs succeeded the Medici in Tuscany, the Este in Modena, and the Sforza in Milan. They succeeded to Venice after the fall of Napoleon, and had ephemeral sovereignties in other Italian territories.[189] These claims were eventually extinguished, the last of them by the unification of Italy (1859-66). But where the Hapsburgs were in control, the double eagle followed. Figure 102, the arms of the (Austrian) Kingdom of Lombardy-Venetia, may serve as a representative of this tendency. Note the heraldic variations on the eagle's breastshield (the viper of Milan and the lion of Venice behind the Austrian genealogical arms) and the Lombard crown that sits above it. Similar variations marked the emblems of other Habsburg territories in Italy.

Figures 114 and 115 are examples of Italian double eagle supporters. The first are the arms of the ancient Sicilian family of the Filangeri, the second those of the Commune of Velletri near Rome.[190] Some Italian noble families bear the double eagle *unmarshalled*, that is, as their arms on an undivided field.[191] The Giustiniani of Venice, for instance, a family claiming connection to the Emperor Justinian, had a double eagle for their arms, but so did other high patrician families. There is even a seal from 1278 showing Count Philip of Savoy with a double eagle on his shield and his horse trappings. See Figure

---

[187] See *id.*, 483.

[188] The term *fount of honor* refers to the sovereign as the originator and sole bestower of honors such as arms, titles, decorations, and orders of chivalry.

[189] For example Sicily, Sardinia and Parma.

[190] In the Velletri arms the legend EST MIHI LIBERTAS PAPALIS ET IMPERALIS means *I have papal and imperial liberty* – until 1589 it was a free city by authority of both powers. The letters S.P.Q.V. in the border around the shield mean *Senate and People of Velletri*, echoing the famous S.P.Q.R. of Rome.

[191] Here too there are many variations. For instance, the Castiglione of Naples bear their traditional family arms (a lion holding a castle) on the breast of a black double eagle on a *green* field.

116.[192] The Marquessate of Montferrat, where a cadet branch of the of the Byzantine imperial family of Palaeologue established itself from 1306 to 1533, made a distinctive quasi-imperial use of the double eagle.[193] Figure 117 is a *scudo d'oro* minted at Casale by Guglielmo II Palaeologue (William IX of Montferrat), who ruled from 1494 to 1518.[194]

Finally there is the *Palio*, a horse-race competition among the *contrade* (wards) of Siena and one of the most famous spectacles in Italy. Each *contrada* has a name and a banner; the banners are colorfully decorated with fantastic designs and symbols. One of the *contrade* is called *Aquila* (eagle). Their banner, an example of which is shown in Figure 118, is yellow with a black double eagle, a design documented as having been given them by Charles V in 1546.[195]

THE DOUBLE EAGLE IN GREECE

The double eagle, as a symbol of Christian independence before the Turkish conquest, was a symbol of national aspiration and achievement in the Balkans (see pages 69-81 below), and this was also true in Greece.[196] But the principal use of the double eagle in Greece, especially since independence, has not been secular but as an emblem of the Greek Orthodox Church.

The Greek Orthodox Church uses the double eagle freely in its iconography and decoration – it is found in churches, and is worn as an ornament by some Orthodox

---

[192]   Philip was related to Baldwin of Constantinople – see pages 41-42 above.

[193]   This cadet dynasty was founded by Theodore Palaeologue, daughter of Empress Eirene, who had been born Yolanda of Montferrat. For more on the Montferrat-Palaeologue connection, see Nicol (1996), note 37, 48-55.

[194]   The name of the coin, *scudo d'oro*, means *golden shield*. The arms on the eagle's breastshield are red over white (*argent, a chief gules*) for Montferrat.

[195]   For more on the Palio banners, with illustrations from every *contrada* over many periods, see Antonio Zazzeroni, *L'Araldica delle Contrade di Siena* [Heraldry of the contradas of Siena] (Florence, 1980). The cypher UI on the breast of the current eagle is a concession from King Umberto I in 1888. *Id.*, 9-10.

[196]   Greece was wrested from Turkish control and established as an independent country in the early 19th century. The First Hellenic Republic was proclaimed in 1822, but the War of Independence was not yet over, and freedom from Turkish suzerainty came in stages, culminating in international recognition of the Kingdom of Greece by the powers in 1832. The original kingdom included only a small part of the present Greek state – for a Wikipedia map showing its gradual increase (and occasional decrease) since then see tinyurl.com/p5jlnmn. The present territory of Greece was not finally defined until 1947.

clergy. It symbolizes the authority of the Ecumenical Patriarch, the chief prelate of the Greek church, resident in Istanbul. In Byzantine days he usually worked closely with the emperor. Figure 119 shows this emblem in stone outside the Patriarch's office in Istanbul.[197] The church flies a yellow flag with the double eagle in black outline – see Figure 120. This flag is also used in the autonomous church-governed so-called Republic of Mount Athos, site of many famous Orthodox monasteries under the authority of the Patriarch; the photograph at right, of a monk hailing a boat by waving the double-eagle flag, was taken at Mount Athos. The eagle is also an international symbol of the church – see for example Figure 121, the emblem of the Greek Orthodox Church in Australia.

In his article "The Shaping of a Symbol – The Double Headed Eagle," Kimon Andreou quotes Archimandrite Zacharias Lianas on the symbolic meaning of the double eagle in the modern Greek Orthodox church.

> After the Fall of Constantinople to the Turks (1453), the Ecumenical Patriarch of Constantinople was recognized by the conqueror Muhammed II as the Ethnarch [national leader] of the Romans. As such, he inherited along with the other imperial symbols (the crown, scepter, robes) the Double-headed Eagle as the symbol of the Nation. This symbol has been used ever since as the emblem of the Ecumenical National Patriarchate and used in the seals of the Patriarchal Bulls. Because of this, it is carved as the Coat of Arms above the gate of the Patriarchal churches. It is also carved on the walls and the floors of the Patriarchal churches and stavropegial monasteries and those houses made stavropegial. It is also conserved on the floors of many temples, among which is the temple of the Metropolis of Mistras. It is embroidered in the Patriarchal clothing and robes. Embroidered on fabrics or tapestries, wherever Constantinople is depicted. In time, whenever a cleric in the jurisdiction of the Ecumenical Patriarchate is ordained and the floor of the particular temple does not have the Double-headed Eagle carved, a tapestry with the symbol is placed under the feet of the ordained to show that he is stepping … on Patriarchal ground, as spiritual subject of the Patriarchate.[198]

---

[197]   The letters OIK Π stand for the Greek for *Ecumenical Patriarchate*. The Greek word *oikoumenē* [οικουμένη] means *the whole world*, and its use in the Patriarch's title is a claim of universal authority. Note St. Peter's keys below the eagle's tail, referencing Jesus' words to Peter in Matthew 16:19: "And I will give unto thee the keys of the kingdom of heaven." The Pope also uses the keys as an emblem.

[198]   From Kimon Andreou's heraldic blogging site ITDG, posted March 27, 2012, at tinyurl.com/mou7v8z. *Archimandrite* is a Greek ecclesiastical title, indicating a priest whose vows have made him eligible to become a bishop. Zacharias Lianas (d. 1952) was head of the

(footnote continues →)

The most important secular use of the double eagle in modern Greece is as an emblem of the army, in black on gold, with a heartshield of the Greek national arms (a white cross on blue). This emblem is seen below on the flag of the Army General Staff; the stripes are green-red-green, with white *fimbriations* between them. The four white stars on the bottom stripe mark it as the personal rank flag of the Chief of Army Staff.[199]

The double eagle is also used (again in black on gold) as the emblem of the Athletic Union of Constantinople, founded in 1924 and now host of a popular football team.[200] And in Figure 122 we see it on the Greek Red Cross Honorary Decoration (gold cross 2d class).[201]

The double eagle appeared as a tiny charge in the ugly and awkward first arms of the Second Greek Republic, in use only from 1924 to 1926.[202] And it featured prominently on the flag of the ephemeral Autonomous Republic of Northern Epirus (1914-16), shown in Figure 123 on

---

(*footnote continues ...*)

Rizarios Hieratic School between 1923 and 1925. A *metropolis* in this context means a city that serves as a regional, provincial or diocesan religious capital. A *stavropegial* monastery is one under the authority of a patriarch [archbishop] or a synod rather than a diocesan bishop (the Mount Athos monasteries are stavropegial).

[199] The picture was taken during a military ceremony, and posted on November 4, 2011, to the Greek National Pride website at tinyurl.com/lotq2xe. The flag and emblem can be seen more clearly on the Greek Army website at tinyurl.com/lkdosbv. The motto on the army emblem, Ελευθερον το Ευψυχον [*eleutheron to eupsychon*], comes from Pericles' eulogy for the Athenian dead (431 BC), reported in Thucydides, *History of the Peloponnesian War*, 2.43.4. The phrase has been rendered as *freely spirited*. The complete line has Pericles telling the citizens of Athens: "Now you yourselves ought to imitate [the fallen] and not avoid the perils of war, considering that freedom is the basis of your happiness and valor of your freedom." Thanks to Professor Tatiana Tsakiropoulou-Summers for this translation.

[200] Called AEK after their Greek initials. See their emblem at Figure 229.

[201] The crown was no longer used on this decoration after the abolition of the Greek monarchy in 1974. See George Stratoudakis, *Greek Medals* (Athens, 2001), 156.

[202] See Wikimedia image at tinyurl.com/m7nuzwg.

one of its stamps.[203] Figure 124 is a coin issued by Cyprus when Makarios, a Greek Orthodox archbishop, was its president.

As a curiosity, Figure 125 shows the elaborate seal of the "House of Lascaris Comnenus of Constantinople," which quaintly claims the Byzantine throne through supposed descent from the Comnenus Dynasty. Their eagle shows marked Austrian influence – note especially what appears to be the "Crown of Charlemagne" on the dexter (left) head of the eagle.[204] I include it to show the continued iconographic power of the Greek double eagle.

THE DOUBLE EAGLE IN RUSSIA

The history of the double eagle as a state symbol in Russia is somewhat clearer than it is for Germany, because it *appears* to start at a known time, with a specific action whose meaning was unambiguous. According to the generally received view, the double eagle became a state symbol in Russia in 1497, when Ivan III (right), called *the Great*, Grand Prince of Moscow, placed it on the reverse of his seal.[205] Figure 126 shows this seal. The

---

[203] The Autonomous Republic of Northern Epirus was proclaimed in 1914 by Greeks in southern Albania, and at the start received some international recognition. But World War I interfered with its permanent establishment, and in 1921 the area was ceded to Albania. The cross above the double eagle on the Northern Epirus stamp corresponds to the star in the Albanian flag of the time, based on the arms of Skanderbeg. See pages 70-73 below.

A few other historic Greek flags with double eagle imagery are illustrated in E. Kokkone and G. Tsiberiotes, *Ellenikes Semaies* [Ελληνικες Σημαιες; Greek flags] (Athens, 1997).

[204] See page 40 and Figure 63. *Dexter*, although it means *right*, as a heraldic term presupposes a viewpoint looking down, as if the viewer were holding the shield or device in front of him. It thus corresponds to the left side of a heraldic composition viewed from the front (as on a printed page). Likewise *sinister*, although meaning *left*, refers to the right side as seen from the front.

[205] The image of Grand Prince Ivan is taken from the *Imperial Book of Titles* (Tsarskiye Titulyarnik, Царский Титулярник), made in a few manuscript copies for imperial use around 1672. It is difficult to assess at this remove whether the portraits of early rulers are fanciful or are based on life studies now lost. The *Tsarskiye Titulyarnik* is also an early source for Russian regional heraldry. It has been published in a two-volume facsimile edited by Y. M. Eskin (Moscow, 2007). For a Wikimedia Commons gallery of 53 portraits from the *Tsarskiye Titulyarnik*, captioned in English, see tinyurl.com/kcbq9uu; see also a gallery of other images from the book at tinyurl.com/lcm9bs3. For a facsimile of the entire work, including other heraldic material but mostly in black and white engravings rather than original paintings, presented in Russian, see tinyurl.com/mk2owx8. A well-illustrated article, somewhat awkward to navigate, appears on the Russian Rarus Gallery website at tinyurl.com/k6v8dka. The image on the front cover of this book comes from the *Tsarskiye Titulyarnik*.

obverse has a scene of St. George killing the dragon, an important image in Russian state iconography. This scene was later moved to the eagle's breastshield.[206]

According to this view, Ivan was using Byzantine imagery taken from the double eagle of the Palaeologue dynasty. When the Turks finally conquered Constantinople in 1453, this left a void in the imagined structure of the world. Ivan hoped to fill this void by establishing his Orthodox Christian empire, just then beginning and based in Moscow, as a "Third Rome" in succession to the previous, now fallen, empires of Rome and Constantinople.[207] To help in this effort, in 1472 he married Princess Sophia Palaeologue, niece of the last Byzantine emperor Constantine XI Palaeologue, and adopted Byzantine forms, symbols and court practices, including the double eagle.

This is not exactly wrong. While we do not know for certain just what was in Prince Ivan's mind in 1497, it is a plausible view. However, earlier double eagle coins were minted for the Grand Duchy of Tver, near to Moscow and an early rival for dominance in the world of post-Mongol Russia.[208] The last two Princes of Tver, Ivan Mikhailovich and Mikhail Borisovich, both issued double eagle coins, a few of which have survived (Figure 127 is a silver *denge* coin of Prince Mikhail). Ivan conquered Tver in 1486, so the last of these coins had to have been issued no later than that year, and their design was certainly known to Ivan.[209] It is therefore reasonable, or at least as reasonable as the Byzantine theory, to suppose that Ivan intended his double eagle to reflect his local hegemony as well as his notional assumption of the leadership of the Orthodox world.[210]

---

[206] The St. George image may have begun as a more generic rider, or been intended as an equestrian image of Ivan himself, as was common in seals of the nobility in Western Europe. Or it may have been an image from an ancient carved gemstone, such as Russian princes and nobles used before the adoption of western-style seals, or something else entirely.

[207] A modern historian epitomized the "Third Rome" ideology this way: "[S]ince the God-ordained Christian Roman empires of Rome and Constantinople had fallen because they had strayed from correct divine will, only the Muscovite Orthodox Russian imperial state rightly could lay claim to the divine mantle of political leadership within the general Orthodox world." Dennis Hupchick, *The Balkans: From Constantinople to Communism* (New York, 2002), 250.

[208] The Mongols of the Golden Horde, who had conquered all the ancient Russian principalities by 1240, were finally beaten back in 1480, and the structure of what became the new Russian Empire began to coalesce.

[209] Similar coins called *pulo* were issued in copper during this period, by Tver and also by Pskov. See the Omnicoin website at tinyurl.com/q4q3vxg for an image of a double eagle *pulo* from Pskov. Figure 128 is an even earlier double-eagle coin, said to have been minted by Jani Beg, a khan of the Mongol Golden Horde (reigned 1342-57).

[210] Indeed the inscription on Ivan's 1497 seal, in a style reminiscent of western imperial forms, identifies him as "Grand Prince Ioan [Ivan] by God's grace sovereign of all Russia and Grand Prince" of nine named territories, including Moscow and Tver. Gustav Alef, "The Adoption of the Muscovite Two-Headed Eagle: A Discordant View," *Speculum* (Cambridge, 1966), 41:1.

It seems likely to me that the 1497 seal carried both intentions.[211]

Gustave Alef, an American scholar, put forth what he called a "discordant" view, arguing that Ivan's seal was inspired by the adoption of the double eagle as an imperial symbol in Germany.[212]

> [T]he Muscovite grand prince, discovering that the Holy Roman Emperor utilized the two-headed eagle on his state seal, while his son and designated successor could only display a single-headed one, replied by adopting a similar device for his own. * * * [S]eals embodying the new device were appended to the letters sent by Ivan III to the Hapsburgs and [were] also … attached to the treaty made with King Maximilian, son of the emperor. This was but one means by which Ivan asserted his equality with [German Emperor] Frederick III. Implicitly this intimates that Ivan III accepted the Byzantine inheritance, though he did not do much else to push the claim in theory or in deed.[213]

It strengthens Alef's theory that no double eagle seal was adopted by Ivan or any other Muscovite prince until 25 years after the Palaeologue marriage, and 17 years after he overthrew the suzerainty of the Golden Horde in 1480.

Whatever the background, after Prince Ivan's adoption of this seal in 1497 the double eagle remained the emblem of the Muscovite grand princes, the Russian emperors, and the post-imperial Russian state to the present day (except for the period of Communist rule, 1918-91). The changes in the eagle were principally in detail. The beaks and tongues were modified to follow Western stylization practices. The image of the rider (later specifically identified as St. George) was moved to a heartshield, and made to face sometimes left, sometimes right. The number and style of the crowns was varied; the arms of provinces, from a early date arrayed around the eagle, came to rest on its wings. Regalia were added, such as the scepter and orb (in its talons) and the chain of the Order of St. Andrew First-Called (around the breastshield). Perhaps most important visually, the posture of the eagle and the elevation of its wings changed with the times. Figures 129-

---

[211] As with the Byzantine double eagle itself, there is some evidence of the use of the double eagle in the area before the mid-15th century. Some folk motifs display shapes that *could* be seen as double eagles; the same could be said of some coins (like that of Jani Beg just mentioned, note 209) issued by the Golden Horde. It is neither necessary nor possible to get to the bottom of this here. Certainly its use by Tver and Pskov did not spring from nowhere, but we are unlikely ever to know if Ivan's eagle was taken just from Byzantium, or had other sources.

[212] Alef, note 210.

[213] *Ibid.*, 3. The entire article is rich in historical detail and repays reading in full. Alef suggests in particular that Ivan adopted the double eagle seal for diplomatic communications with Frederick, in order to assert his imperial status (and to have it accepted), after Frederick's inept ambassador insulted Ivan by suggesting the marriage of Ivan's daughter to a German magnate of inferior rank. *Id.*, 14-15, note 39.

131, taken from coins, illustrate a few variations.[214] None of these changes altered the essential nature of the display.[215] A lovely example of the final (1857) pattern appears on the inside back cover of this book.[216]

The double eagle was the main emblem of the tsars and the imperial regime, and figured on countless objects of display. At right is a herald from the Russian Order of the White Eagle (showing the white eagle of Poland on the black double eagle of Russia). Figure 132 is a woodcut of the arms of Moscow, from the Slavonic Bible (1663). Figures 133-135 show items of more recent date: a *jeton* of the Moscow Technical School,[217] the badge of the Order of St. Andrew, and a helmet of the Life Guards Regiment.[218] The double eagle figured very heavily in the highly artificial top-down system of civic heraldry under the tsarist regime – Figure 136 gives a typical example, the 1796 arms of the town of Chudovo. Figure 137 is a colour-staff from a Russian guards regiment.

---

[214] For an exhaustive illustrated catalogue of the varieties of double eagles on Russian coins, see Vasily Uzdenikov, *Heraldic Appearance of Russian Coins 1700-1917* (Moscow, 1998) (bilingual English and Russian).

[215] For a detailed stage-by-stage review of the development of the double eagle on Russian state seals, many superb color pictures of Russian state heraldry and heraldic display, seals, flags, objects of art, and much else, see G. V. Vilinbakov, *The State Coat of Arms of Russia: 500 Years* (St. Petersburg, 1997), 24. This valuable and beautifully produced bilingual (Russian-English) work was a joint production of the Hermitage Museum and the Russian State Heraldry Office.

[216] The arms on the wings are (counter-clockwise from top left): Kazan, Poland, Tauric Chersonese [Crimea], the ancient polities of Kiev, Vladimir and Novgorod (marshalled on a single shield), Finland, Georgia, Siberia and Astrakhan. This model was adopted under the influence of the German heraldist Bernhard Karl, Freiherr von Koehne (1817-1866).

[217] A *jeton* is a small badge, usually made of gold or silver and enamel, indicating membership in a military unit, a civilian organization, or a school class. It is something like an American fraternity pin or nursing badge. Jetons were very popular in Tsarist Russia and hundreds, perhaps thousands, of varieties are known. They are an exceptionally abundant source of Russian heraldic and state symbolism. The most exhaustive and well-illustrated catalogue to have text in English is V. V. Sanko, *Chest Regiment Badges of Russia* (Moscow, 2002) and its companion *Decorations and Memorial Badges of Russia* (Moscow, 2003). For a less overwhelming treatment in English, see Robert Wehrlich and Serge Adolenko, *Badges of Imperial Russia* (Washington, 1972) and Robert Wehrlich, *Jetons of Imperial Russia* (Washington, 1985).

[218] The Hermitage Museum label for this object identifies it not as a real helmet, but as a silver goblet made in the shape of one (presumably for the regimental mess).

Figure 138 is a Russian military guidon from the 17th century. Figure 139 shows a typical Russian regimental flag of the late 18th century, German in inspiration; the double eagle was at the center of many of these.[219] The exuberant colonel's colour of an artillery regiment is seen in Figure 140. Figure 141 is a standard pattern infantry colour of the period of the Napoleonic Wars – the tints varied according to the region where the regiment was raised.[220] Figure 142, the flag of an imperial envoy, is representative of a wide variety of Russian official flags featuring the double eagle.[221] Figure 143 is the imperial standard for use afloat – note that the eagle is holding in its beaks and talons maps of the seas supposedly subject to Russian naval power.[222] A ceremonial state standard, with a total of 51 heraldic fields (some territorial, some dynastic), appears in Figure 145.

The Provisional Government, which operated (barely) between the fall of the Empire in 1917 and the accession of the Soviet government in 1918, used a seal with a naked double eagle, all regalia and attributes removed (Figure 144).[223] But this ephemeral image was swept away with the Soviet Revolution, the adoption of anti-heraldic emblems (on the Communist side – the eagle survived a bit longer on the counter-revolutionary side), and the establishment of the Soviet Union in 1922.

---

[219]   The flag illustrated is the colour of the Ryazan Regiment of Carabineers. For a magnificent collection of Russian military and naval flags for this whole period, in a series of hundreds of water colors, captioned in French as well as Russian, see Vladimir Zvegintsov, *Znamena i Shtandarti Russkoye Armee XVI vek – 1914 i Morskiye Flagi* [Flags and standards of the Russian army, 16th century – 1914, and naval flags] (Moscow, 2008). T. Shevyakov, in his *Flags and Standards of the Russian Imperial Army of the Late 19th/Early 20th Centuries* (Colorado Springs, 2007), 3, says Zvegintsov's book "understandably contain[s] many inaccuracies and mistakes since the author was unable to work in Soviet archives." Even so, it is remarkably beautiful and is by far the best and most comprehensive work with captions in a Western European language.

[220]   The basic design of this pattern – a *paty* cross (that is, a cross with angled arms terminating in flat ends) is a German design for military colours. There were many variations of color, number of arms, balance of arms and field, figured partition lines, etc.

[221]   Vladimir A. Sokolov, *Flagi Rossiyeskoye Imperiye i CCCP v Dokumentach* [Flags of the Russian Empire and USSR in documents] (Moscow, 2001), gives a very thorough history of all the official patterns back through the 19th century and some from earlier, with documents, dates, and black and white illustrations.

[222]   The Baltic, White, Black and Caspian Seas. This pattern of standard was first used by Peter the Great in 1703. See Vilinbakov, note 215, 40. Russian flag practice, as well as the present Dutch-based tricolor and many other features, date from Tsar Peter's *incognito* visit to Western Europe (and especially the Netherlands) in what was called his "Grand Embassy" in 1697-98.

[223]   Similar naked treatment was given the *Reichsadler* in Germany after the fall of the Second German Empire in 1918.

In 1990 the Soviet Union began to disintegrate. Lithuania was the first part to secede, in March; in June the Russian Federation, the largest and most important of the Soviet "republics," declared sovereignty over its territory, which included the Russian heartland.

In November 1990 Russian authorities began work a new flag and coat of arms. After much intense discussion and debate, the proposal to restore the double eagle, complete with crowns, scepter, orb and heartshield of St. George (but not the wing-shields or the  order-collar), was adopted in a decree by President Boris Yeltsin (1931-2007) (right) on November 30, 1993. See Figure 146. It was one of the most dramatic reversals in the history of heraldic expression.[224] Figure 148 is the current (1994 pattern) Russian presidential standard.

Showing the continued vitality of the double eagle as a symbol of Russia, when separatists sympathetic to Russia proclaimed an "independent people's republic" in the Ukrainian city of Donetsk in April 2014, the flag they produced for their supposed state was a tricolor with a double eagle (Figure 149).[225]

THE DOUBLE EAGLE IN THE BALKANS

The double eagle figures prominently in the modern flags of three Balkan countries: Albania, Serbia and Montenegro. All three countries, which had once been part of the Christian Byzantine hinterland, were conquered by the Turks and lived for centuries under Turkish control. All three had traditions of resistance under warlords who bore a double eagle, presumably Byzantine in inspiration. It is difficult for me, with the resources available to me and no facility in Albanian or Slavic languages, to assess how accurate these traditions really are.[226] But the traditions themselves, which go back centuries, may be sufficient for present purposes.

---

[224]   Some of the internal debate is recounted in Vilinbakov, note 215, 52-56. The State Bank of Russia uses the naked double eagle, which may be seen on current Russian coins – see Figure 147.

[225]   The Donetsk tricolor is black-red-blue instead of the white-red-blue of Russia, and the eagle has an icon of St. Michael on its breast. Thanks to Peter Orensky for this image, vectorized from press photographs. For more on this flag, see the Flags of the World website at tinyurl.com/l946tev. Kharkov had a similar design for its separatist flag, with green, blue and red horizontal stripes – for an image by Zoltan Horvath see *id.* at tinyurl.com/m9ynd2c.

[226]   The guidance of Alexander Soloviev was especially useful here – see note 6.

In Albania the story begins with Gjerj [George] Kastrioti (1405-1468) (left), son of Gjon [John], head of the small Albanian principality of Kastrioti.[227] Gjerj was given to the Ottomans as a hostage, became a Moslem, and made a career in the Ottoman army. He is known in history as Skanderbeg after his title *Iskander Bey* [Lord Alexander] gained in Ottoman service. In 1443 Kastrioti deserted from the Turkish forces, became a Christian again, and launched an Albanian resistance army that defeated the Ottomans in many battles. But in 1478, ten years after he died, the Ottomans finally subdued the Albanians and maintained their dominion there until modern times.

Skanderbeg is said to have raised a double eagle flag in his resistance army, and this flag (called in Albanian *Flamur e Skënderbeut*) is said to have been based on his arms.[228] There is no reason to doubt this story, which is attested to not long after Skanderbeg's lifetime.[229] Jaho Brahaj, in his book on the Albanian flag, reprints what appears to be a modern redrawing of a seal attributed to Skanderbeg (Figure 150) – the letters D AL supposedly standing for *Dominus Albaniae* [Lord of Albania].[230] If authentic this seal would go a long way toward supporting the flag story.[231]

---

[227] The Greek legend in the picture reads, on the left, Ὁ Ἀετος [the eagle], and on the right Γεώργιος Καστριώτης [Georgios Kastriotes].

[228] It is at least as likely, in an area not then fully Western in culture, that his arms were based on the flag.

[229] Jaho Brahaj, *Flamuri i Kombit Shqiptar* [Flag of the Albanian nation] (Tiranë, 2002), 100, cites Marinus Barletius, *Historia de Vita et Gestis Scanderbegi Epirotarum Principis* [History of the life and acts of Skanderbeg, Prince of Epirus] (Rome, 1506). He quotes Barletius as follows: *Rubea vexilla nigris et bicipitibus distincta aquilis gerebat Scanderbecus* [Scanderbeg bore a red flag with a distinctive two-headed black eagle]. See Figure 153. Eyewitnesses to Skanderbeg's campaigns could still have been alive in 1506. Brahaj also cites an anonymous work called *Anonimi i Tivarit*, published in Venice in 1480, the original now lost but republished in Brescia in 1742. *Id.*, 146-7. I cannot assess the accuracy of this earlier source, but if it does describe Skanderbeg's flag as red and black, that is probably as close in time and place to the events themselves as we can get.

[230] Brahaj, note 229, p. 91, no. 2.

[231] Soloviev (1935), note 6, 153-4, mentions an Albanian magnate of the previous (14th) century, Andrea II Musachi, who appears also to have borne as an emblem a double eagle with a star above, in token of his having been made a *despot*, presumably by the Byzantine emperor (see

(footnote continues →)

Later sources show a coat of arms for the Castrioti family, as Italian nobles, that follows the design on this seal (with a star appearing on a *pile*, a triangular form descending from the top of the shield) – see Figure 151. The family arms are shown with the pile, but in black on gold, in the 16th century Korenić-Neorić and Fojnički armorials.[232] As these armorials date from after Skanderbeg's time, they are not direct evidence of what he actually used.[233] They are suggestive, though, without being dispositive, and do not support the unusual color combination – a black eagle on red – that has been followed without exception for Albanian flags in modern times, with the tradition that it was used in former times also.[234] But the earlier testimony of Bartelius is persuasive – I note also that black on red was a favorite color scheme for Byzantine silks.

Independence-minded groups agitated against the Ottomans during the 19th century; the first of many modern revolts began in 1833. Independence agitators are reported to have carried a red-and-black double-eagle "Flag of Skanderbeg," and that flag was raised at the abortive proclamation of independence at Mrdita in 1911[235] and again at the slightly more enduring proclamation at Vlorë in 1912 (see photograph below).

(*footnote continues ...*)

page 20 above). We probably do not need to get to the bottom of this story, so full of ifs, beyond noting the *possibility* of a double-eagle forerunner to Skanderbeg.

[232] The Korenić-Neorić Armorial is a 1595 copy of a slightly earlier work, now lost; the Fojnički Armorial, has a spurious internal date of 1340, but is really from about 100 years after after the Korenić-Neorić. For an expandable facsimile of the Korenić-Neorić, see the Serbian website Грбовник Коренић-Неорић [Korenić-Neorić Armorial] at tinyurl.com/lmj3xvk. For a facsimile of the Fojnički Armorial, see the the (Bosnian) Camo Ceja website at tinyurl.com/2ulfeo8. The Fojnički has been published in many modern editions, including (in English and Bosnian) as Franjo Miletić and Dubravko Lovrenović, *Fojnicki Grbovnik* [Fojnicki armorial] (Sarajevo, 2005).

[233] A reasonably reliable modern source gives this same pattern, in black on gold with blue pile, as the arms of the present Neapolitan noble family of Castrioti Skanderbegh. See *Elenco Storico*, note 186, 125. Skanderbeg was given two seignories in the Neapolitan Kingdom in 1463 as a reward for military assistance there; he was also enrolled as a Venetian noble. For a brief but interesting account of the Neapolitan House of Castrioti Skanderbegh, see "The Castriota Family," on the Heraldica website at tinyurl.com/la93otk.

[234] Black on red is unusual because of difficulties in visibility. These difficulties are the reason heraldry usually insists that charges in dark colors (red, black, blue, green) appear only on light fields (yellow, white) and *vice versa*. In Ottoman times Albanian vessels owned by non-Moslems were allowed a red flag with a black stripe. Perhaps these colors inspired the modern color combination, or perhaps (more likely) they followed national colors in use at the time – Greek ships had a blue stripe. See the discussion by Jaume Ollé on the Flags of the World website at tinyurl.com/mp2g72z.

[235] See the article on Terenzio Tocci in Robert Elsie, ed., *A Biographical Dictionary of Albanian History* (New York, 2012), 442.

71

Albania had a complicated constitutional history after achieving recognition as an independent state in 1912. Figure 152 is a reconstruction of the 1914 flag of the Principality of Albania, established for Prince Wilhelm von Wied (Prince Vili I), whose ephemeral 1914 sovereignty over Albania, originally sponsored by the European powers, collapsed at the start of World War I.[236] Prince Vili's personal standard is shown as Figure 154.[237]

Every Albanian regime since independence has used the red flag with the black double eagle in one form or another. Some (echoing the Castrioti arms) placed a star above the eagle (white in early years, yellow under the Communists). Some regimes put the so-called Crown of Skanderbeg (a helmet topped with an antelope's head) over the eagle – this was favored by King Zog, who reigned 1928-39.[238] The puppet kingdom under the Italians (1939-45) removed the helmet but added fasces and Savoyard emblems.[239] Since 1992, after the fall of the Communist regime, the eagle on the national flag has had no

---

[236]   This flag design, based on the then-recently-revived *Flamur e Skënderbeut*, was commissioned by Prince William from the distinguished German heraldic artist Emil Doepler the Younger. See discussion on the Flags of the World website at tinyurl.com/krmwhvv. The lightning bolts were Doepler's innovation. For other examples of Doepler's work, see Figures 64 and 83.

[237]   On the prince's standard, as reconstructed by Jaume Ollé, the Doepler eagle has a heraldic crown (without a cross at the top, Albania being largely Moslem) and a breastshield with the arms of Wied (gold with a peacock in natural colors facing outward). Wied was a very small German state, divided into even smaller parts (Wilhelm was a prince of Wied-Neuwied), and *mediatized* in 1804 by being folded into Nassau when the last reigning prince refused to join Napoleon's Confederation of the Rhine. A mediatized principality loses its sovereignty, but its princes retain their status, useful for royal marriages and for appointment to the occasional vacant Balkan throne. For a summary of the intricate constitutional history of Wied, see the article "Fürstentum Wied" on German Wikipedia at tinyurl.com/n6xjkcz.

[238]   Ahmet Zogu (born Zogolli) (1895-1961) was a signer of the Declaration of Albanian Independence in 1912, and held a series of increasingly important posts in the chaotic governments that preceded the first Albanian Republic, established in 1925 under Zogu's presidency. He made himself King Zog in 1928, and went into exile after being overthrown by the Italians in 1939. The Crown of Skanderbeg is a real object, now in the Treasury [*Schatzkammer*] of the Hofburg [Imperial Palace] in Vienna – for a picture of it see Wikimedia Commons at tinyurl.com/pxwxk6f. A somewhat better picture, with many other images of Skanderbeg but little context, appears on the Albanian Library blogsite at tinyurl.com/pfexanb.

[239]   For a good collection of these and other variations on the *Flamur e Skënderbeut*, with historical context, see "Flag History of Albania" on the Ozoutback website at tinyurl.com/k6vh3ps.

additional emblem – the national flag with the modern Albanian eagle's distinctive round-tipped feathers and squarish wing mass is shown in Figure 155.[240] Figure 156 is the arms in current use (the helmet has been restored). Figure 157, an Albanian revenue stamp of 1920, gives the eagle a jaunty art deco treatment. Figure 158, a gold coin from 1927 (minted in Italy) is one of the most beautifully realized renditions of the double eagle made in the last century (or maybe ever).[241]

The largely Albanian population of Kosovo raised the Albanian flag as their separatist symbol, and (with the eagle close to the hoist) for their unrecognized Republic of Kosova. They tried to use it as a national flag when the United Nations intervened to form a *de facto* protectorate (protecting the Kosovars from the Serbs who insisted on sovereignty over Kosovo, based on its incorporation into the former Yugoslavia). But the United Nations would not permit this blatantly nationalistic emblem, and insisted on an anodyne flag with a map-based device instead. Albanian minorities inside Serbia and other Balkan countries persist in trying to use the black double eagle on red, usually encountering official resistance.[242]

SERBIA

Serbia in our period emerged as an independent state under the Nemanjić Dynasty that Stephan Nemanja founded in the 12th century and that ruled, more or less, until 1371. As a Christian country in the Balkan hinterland of the Byzantine (and Ottoman) empires, Serbia was alternately (and sometimes simultaneously) a rival, vassal, ally and opponent of Byzantium, and its ruling dynasty was in close communication with the emperors. It became a powerful, if ephemeral, medieval empire, reaching its zenith under Stephan Dushan the Mighty, King of Serbia from 1331 to 1355. After Stephan Dushan died his state disintegrated, but was revived in a different form by a successor (Lazarević) dynasty, which ruled until Serbia's independence was lost at the Battle of Kosovo in 1389, and afterward as a Turkish vassal until 1459.

The medieval use of the Serbian double eagle seems well attested from contemporary sources. It appears near Belgrade on the 1339 map of the Genoese (or maybe Catalan) cartographer Angelino Dulcert – see Figure 159. A double eagle appears on the early

---

[240]   In Figures 152 and 154-6 the background has been lightened – dark red and black provide insufficient contrast for easy recognition in black-and-white reproduction.

[241]   Note especially the spread of the feathers in the wings and the tail, and the delicate interactions between the legs and tail, and between the wingtips and the surrounding lettering.

[242]   In Serbia, for example, it is illegal to use an organization flag identical to the flag of a foreign country.

14th century ring of Queen Teodora, mother of Stephan Dushan (Figure 160).[243] Prior use is known from images and relics – "from the earliest years of the 13th century," wrote the Serbian historian Alexander Soloviev, "we observe a very intense diffusion of the double eagle into Slavic lands."[244] Figure 161 is a drawing of a fresco of the 12th-century Prince Miroslav of Hum, in what is now Montenegro, wearing a Byzantine-style robe decorated with double-eagle medallions.[245] Other such frescoes and reliefs survive from the 13th-15th centuries, showing other Serbian princes similarly vested.[246] Figure 162 is a metal decoration from a chandelier in the Markov monastery, in Skopje in what is now Macedonia, built by Vukašin Mrnjavčević (briefly "King of the Serbs and Greeks") and completed around 1366 – note the cross between the eagle's heads.[247] Examples could be multiplied.[248]

The vestments in the frescoes show the eagle in Byzantine gold on red, but the double eagle also appears for the Nemanjić dynasty in white on red in later documents such as the Korenić-Neorić (Figure 164) and Fojnički Armorials. The double eagle also stands as the arms of Stephan Lazarević in Ulrich Richenthal's *Constanzer Chronik* (Figure

---

[243]   Alexander Soloviev, *Istoria Srpskog Grba* [History of the Serbian Arms] (Belgrade, 1958), plate 24, no. 3, dates the ring between 1320 and 1330. He writes elsewhere (note 6, 139), "it is difficult to say if [the eagle] was borne as a sign of her Bulgarian imperial origin or as an emblem of her Serbian royal status" (tr. DFP).

[244]   Soloviev (1935), note 6, 137 (tr. DFP).

[245]   He holds a model of the church he founded in Bijelo Polje, site of the fresco.

[246]   Soloviev (1935), note 6, 137-140, discusses many of these frescoes from the 13th century on. For color images of two of them, see Wikimedia Commons at tinyurl.com/lh5zksf (fresco of Prince Lazar Hrebeljanović (1329-1389) in the Ravanica Monastery in central Serbia (detail, but including an eagle roundel)), and at tinyurl.com/mwmnllf (fresco of his son Prince Stephan Lazarević (1374-1427) in Manasija Monastery). As in Byzantine practice, the double eagle on court robes appears to be associated with the office of despot. Stephan Lazarović was made a despot by Emperor Manuel II in 1402 (see Soloviev, note 6, 142), and thereafter this title was associated with the Serbian throne. But Stephan Dushan's commander Jovan Oliver Grčinić, a despot and a sebastocrator, is shown garbed in double-eagle robes without any suggestion that he was a sovereign.

[247]   It is possible that the chandelier is from a later date than the original monastery.

[248]   For example Soloviev (1958), note 243, plate 23, nos. 2-6, shows five double-eagle roundels.

Bulgarian Emperor Michael Shishman (Mihail Asen III, ruled 1323-30) also used a double eagle on his coins (Figure 163). See Nikola Moushmov, *Ancient Coins of the Balkan Peninsula and the Coins of the Bulgarian Monarchs* (Sofia, 1912), available in English translation on the Wildwinds website at tinyurl.com/moe46j9. The double-eagle coins are shown on plates 54 and 57 (links in the article). It appeared on other medieval Bulgarian coins too – see Soloviev (1935), note 6, 144-5. Bosnian rulers of the 15th century also put a double eagle on their seals. See *id.*, 143-44.

165),[249] and as the arms of Serbia (and of the Nemanjić) in the *Stematografija* of 1741 (Figure 167).[250] These early uses make it more reliable to guess that the white double eagle on red served as a national as well as a dynastic symbol before the Ottoman conquest, and afterwards as a symbol of resistance to it. There seems no reason to doubt that the double eagle as a symbol was traditionally associated with pre-Ottoman Christian regimes in Serbian territory.

The principal symbol of the Serbian nation during the Ottoman period was the so-called *Serbian cross*, a white Greek (that is, equal-armed) cross with white *ocila* [оцила] in each corner. The word *ocila* is usually translated *firesteels*, after a similarly shaped antique device for striking on flint to raise a spark for fire-making. But in fact these symbols are ornate versions of the Greek letter B, and the Serbian cross is really the old Byzantine tetragrammatic cross referencing a Palaeologue slogan (see pages 23-24 above).[251] The *ocila* have appeared in various forms over the centuries (for example, as noted, the Seville Franciscan called them *links*).

The First Serbian Uprising in 1804 (against the Ottoman Turks) led to an ephemeral Serbian state (1804-13) under George Petrović, known in history as *Karageorge* [Black George].[252] He was the founder of the Karageorgević dynasty, which alternated with the Obrenović dynasty (often by murder) until 1945 in ruling the post-Ottoman Serbian state. Significantly, though, while the double eagle appeared on Karageorge's seal (Figure 168), it does not appear in the government seal adopted at that time.[253]

---

[249]   Richenthal, note 112, p. 108v. The German legend identifies him as *Dispolt zu Ratzen*, meaning *Despot of Rascia*, one of the core territorial elements of Serbia. As noted, this 1483 work purported to show the heraldic situation in 1415. The two horns Richenthal shows on the shield may have been a misunderstanding of a horned helmet borne as a crest – see Figure 172.

[250]   The *Stematografija* is the earliest printed work of Balkan heraldry. It was reprinted in facsimile at K. Žefarović, ed., *Izobrazhenij Oruzhij Iliricheskikh: Stematografija* (Novi Sad, 1961). Soloviev (1935), note 6, 137, theorizes that the Nemanjić double eagle on a 13th century fresco could be explained by the relationship between the Nemanjić and the Comneni. For citations to the two Balkan armorials, see note 232. Another image from the *Stematografija* appears on page 139.

[251]   An alternate narrative, deriving these symbols from the Cyrillic letter C (equivalent to the Latin S), referencing a Serbian slogan Само Слога Србина Спасава [*Samo Sloga Srbina Spasava*; *Only unity saves the Serbs*], said to be the creation of the national saint St. Sava [Nemanjić], seems certainly a much later invention.

[252]   I am simplifying the spelling of *Karageorge*. According to accepted transliterations of the Serbian word in its original Cyrillic script [Карађорђе], I should perhaps write *Karadjeordje* or even *Karađorđe*.

[253]   It appearance on Karageorge's seal supports the idea that the double eagle was a folk image associated with a Serbian national and religious resistance to Turkish rule under medieval

(footnote continues →)

The First Uprising and its state were suppressed by the Ottomans in 1813, but in 1815 there was a Second Uprising, this one led by Miloš Obrenović. He succeeded in negotiating an autonomous Principality of Serbia, with himself as hereditary prince. But Serbian flags of that time used the Serbian cross (with *ocila*) on a shield as a national emblem, instead of the eagle, sometimes with sovereign trappings such as crowns and robes of estate.[254] The shield was placed on the Serbian tricolor of red, blue and white, the exact reverse of the Russian tricolor.[255] Serbian military flags of this period do not use the white eagle either, although some of them did use the Russian black double eagle on the reverse.[256]

Serbia became completely independent of Turkey in 1878, following a successful war, and was elevated to a kingdom in 1882. On becoming king, Milan I Obrenović (left), adopted new arms for the state, this time including a white double eagle with the Serbian cross on a breastshield. See Figure 169.[257] From that time forward the double eagle with the Serbian cross formed the arms of the Serbian kingdom.

The 1882 flag series included three progressively more complex versions. The civil ensign (used by private merchant ships, and otherwise as a national emblem) had the crowned eagle on the tricolor. The state flag (for government use) added a robe of estate – see Figure 170. The war flag presented a full

(footnote continues …)

    dynasties. There seems no other reason for its adoption by Karageorge, who was not an aristocrat with family arms.

254   A *robe of estate* is a hybrid heraldic image, denoting sovereignty, somewhere between a fur-lined robe and a tent. See Figure 171.

255   This reference to the Russian flag was a gesture to Pan-Slavic feeling, both to satisfy local sentiment and because Serbia needed a Russian alliance to preserve its independence from Austria. Thanks to Željko Heimer for pointing out that the stripes on the Serbian flag of 1835 were red-white-blue.

256   See examples illustrated in Dragana Samarjich, *Vojne Zastave Srba do 1918* [Serbian military flags before 1918] (Belgrade, 1983), and on the Serbian pages of the Flags of the World website.

257   Like their rivals the Karageorgević, the Obrenović were not aristocrats, so it seems likely (although I can't prove it) that their adoption of the double eagle came from the same retrospective impulse mentioned in note 253. In the rendition of the Serbian royal arms in Figure 169, by the Swedish heraldic artist Agi Lindegren (1899), the border around the heartshield is decorative only.

achievement, with a robe of estate *and* supporters and subsidiary banners – amid all that panoply the eagle itself, and its breastshield, were scarcely visible.[258]

The Obrenović dynasty sometimes augmented the eagle by putting the Serbian cross shield in an oval framed by a crowned serpent devouring its own tail.[259] On the cross itself they put an upright sword, and on the cross-members the dates 1389 and 1817.[260] Below the eagle, but within the robe of estate, they put a motto translated as *Time and My Right*.[261] See Figure 171.

Serbia fought on the winning side in World War I; its regimental flags were tricolors with the white eagle on a large red disk (right). The Austro-Hungarian Empire, on the losing side, was dismembered after World War I. There emerged from that ruin a new state for the southern Slavs. It united the short-lived State of Slovenes, Croats and Serbs, *and* the pre-existing states of Serbia and Montenegro, into a new, inversely named Kingdom of Serbs, Croats and Slovenes, under the Karageorgević dynasty that had ruled Serbia before the war. This state also used the crowned double eagle, but altered the breastshield to include fields for Croatia and Slovenia. See Figure 174. It too had a version with a  robe of estate, and a different version of the eagle for royal use (see Figure 173).[262] The

---

[258]   Heraldically these would be the *small, middle, and great arms*. All three flags can be seen, in carefully reconstructed renderings by Mario Febretto, on the Kingdom of Serbia page on the Flags of the World website at <u>tinyurl.com/krean5h</u>.

[259]   The self-devouring serpent, *Ouroboros*, is an ancient alchemical symbol of circularity and immortality. It is tempting, although I can't prove it, to see a connection between the Obrenović serpent and the arms of Prince Stephan Lazarović shown as a Knight of the Dragon. See Figure 172. The Order of the Dragon was a chivalric order founded by King Sigismund of Hungary (later emperor) in 1408 to aid in military resistance to the Turks; Prince Stephan was a founding member.

[260]   The date 1389 recalls the Battle of Kosovo, the last epic battle for Serbian independence before the eventual Ottoman takeover (both armies were nearly annihilated in the battle, but the Ottomans had the resources to recover and the Serbs did not). In 1817 autonomy was restored under the agreement with Prince Milos Obrenović, following the Second Uprising.

[261]   Време и Моје Право [Vreme i Moye Pravo]. Compare the English royal motto *Dieu et Mon Droit* [God and My Right].

[262]   The checky field on both state and royal shields are the ancient arms of Croatia. The crescent and three stars in the state arms stood for Slovenia; the eagle in the third field of the royal arms stood for Krain (in English *Carniola*). The eagle for Krain had only one head.

royal eagle had a new heraldic crown, designed on the model of a Byzantine *kamelaukion*.[263]

In 1929 the state was renamed Yugoslavia, which means *Land of the South Slavs*. The postwar state used the double eagle not only in its basic merchant, state and military flags, but in a whole range of subsidiary official and rank flags.[264] Figure 175 is the lovely 1937 royal standard. Figure 176 is the badge of the Serbian Order of the White Eagle – Yugoslavia had a similar order.

After World War II, and a nasty civil war between Tito's Communist partisans and the remnants of the royal army (who used the white double eagle as a cap badge), the Communists prevailed, and the white eagle disappeared from Serbian and Yugoslav state imagery until 2004, well into the breakup of Yugoslavia into its pre-union constituent parts.[265] A transitional union of Serbia and Montenegro used a white double eagle with a new breastshield, until it too came apart (Figure 177). Since 2004 Serbia has used flags and arms very similar to the old royal Serbian flags, including the crown (republics as well as kingdoms sometimes use a crown to denote sovereignty). Figure 178 shows the current national flag; Figure 179 is the Serbian presidential standard. Figure 180 is the reverse of the colour of the Serbian Air Force, with a slightly new pattern of eagle; Figure 181 is the town flag of Leskovac, a typical modern double-eagle Serbian civic flag.[266]

Serbian nationalist parties in the rest of the former Yugoslavia also display the white eagle; the Serbian portion of the federal state of Bosnia and Herzegovina (*Republika Srpska*) did too until in 2006 its federal Constitutional Court declared it unconstitutional. The *graffito* in Figure 182, and its cancellation by another hand, show the strong feelings that remain in that part of the world after the savage wars accompanying Yugoslavia's disintegration.

---

[263] A *heraldic crown* is a crown designed for heraldic display, but not corresponding to an actual worldly object.

[264] There were two suites of flags, one established by the flag law of 1922 and the other by the law of 1937. See the explanation by Željko Heimer on the Flags of the World website at tinyurl.com/lb8had4.

[265] The Communists did use the four *ocila* as part of their state symbols for Serbia, leaving out the cross – this arrangement continued in use until 2004.

[266] The Serbian Radical Party flies a blue flag with a white outline double eagle holding swords. For an image by Ivan Sarajčić, see the Flags of the World website at tinyurl.com/q5x3bl8.

The two modern nations of Serbia and Montenegro share a common medieval history in the career of Stefan Nemanja (1113-1199) and his successors in the Nemanjić Dynasty. As noted (see pages 74-75), the Nemanjić arms were a white Byzantine-inspired double eagle on red. In 1455 the Nemanjić were succeeded in what is now Montenegro by a new dynasty, the Crnojević, which continued the use of the double eagle. Soloviev refers to a golden double-eagle seal used by Ivan I Crnojević in granting a charter to a monastery in 1485.[267] Figure 183 is the double eagle from the heading page of a book printed in Cetinje in 1494, at the printing house founded there by Đurađ Crnojević, last prince of this dynasty.[268]

As elsewhere in the Balkans, the Turks finally won the struggle; Christian Montenegro disappeared into the Turkish Empire in 1496, with brief periods of autonomy.[269] Montenegro re-emerged from Turkish domination 200 years later, in 1696, under a dynasty called the Petrović-Njegoš, whose rulers used the title prince-bishop [*vladika*]. With Russian protection and political help, the prince-bishops ruled Montenegro as a *de facto* autonomous principality. They assumed the title of prince and sovereign [*knjaz i gospodar*] in 1852, and promoted themselves to king [*kralj*] in 1878, after the European powers recognized their independence at the first Congress of Berlin. All this time the Petrović-Njegoš continued the use of the double eagle, with various adjustments.[270] I *speculate* that this was partly due to the use of the double eagle by previous Christian

---

[267]   Soloviev (1935), note 6, 154. Ivan I married into the family of Serbian despot Stefan Branković – the relationship between the double eagle and the despotic title, even when only by marriage or descent, has already been mentioned.

[268]   It was the first state printing house in the world. The *Oktoih Prvoglasnik* [First Voice] psalter, from which the illustration is taken, was the first book printed anywhere in Cyrillic script.

[269]   The local name for this country is *Crna Gora*, meaning *Black Mountain*; *Montenegro* is an Italian translation first used by the Venetians in whose Adriatic hinterland the country was located.

[270]   For example, the double eagle was reduced to a breastshield in some periods, with other elements forming the outer shield, or the eagle was placed above the shield in a position corresponding more or less to a crest. See the valuable article "Montenegrin State and Dynastic Arms" on the Digital Library of Montenegrin Culture website at tinyurl.com/lhkhev4, which has many illustrations not available elsewhere. While I cannot vouch for the accuracy of this source in every detail, I am persuaded that its general overview is correct. Many examples of double-eagle seals of the prince-bishops are reproduced in Jovan B. Markush, *Grbovi, Zastave i Chymne i Istorija Crne Gora* [Грбови, Заставе и химне у Историји Црне Горе; *Arms, flags and anthems in Montenegrin history*] (Cetinje, 2007), 25-29. The double-eagle design, claimed to be the arms of the prince-bishops around 1711 and reproduced on Wikimedia Commons at tinyurl.com/ldoq3u7, seems poorly attested.

dynasties, and partly in compliment to the Russians whose continued protection was essential to the measure of independence Montenegro had in those years.

Vladika Petar I (ruled 1782-1830)[271] added a lion to his arms, and in the next reign (Petar II) the lion was borne alone on a shield on the double eagle's breast.[272] The lion usually appeared in gold, on a green base, against a blue background, but a green (grassy) base (*compartment*) and blue sky were common features of the pictorial style of Balkan heraldry and need not be seen as fixed – indeed these colors fluctuated over the course of time. One of the first "modern," Western-style iterations of the new Montenegrin arms appeared on the Montenegrin Medal of Bravery, struck by order of Petar II in 1841 (Figure 184). Figure 185 is the arms of Montenegro, published in 1899 by Avi Lindegren – there is no compartment on the breastshield. But compare, for example, the gold 100-perper coin of Nicholas I (1910), where there is one (Figure 186).

The Serbian version of the pan-Slavic colors (red, blue and white) came into use in Montenegro in the 19th century – Srdjan Kalanj writes that Prince Danilo I (ruled 1851-60) (left) hoisted the first one outside his villa in Prcanj in 1860.[273] The color of the eagle fluctuated between white and gold. Although the original eagles of the Crnojević may have been gold on red in the Byzantine style, 19th century reports call the eagle white, or silver, a description fixed in Montenegro's 1905 constitution. On a surviving flag from the 19th century, the eagle is definitely white – see Figure 187.

Montenegro kept its separate nationality and symbols until it was involuntarily merged into the new South Slav kingdom (later Yugoslavia) after World War I. Yugoslavia used essentially Serbian symbols, only slightly modified, and the distinctively Montenegrin eagle disappeared from use until 1993, when it was restored (in white) within the union with Serbia (Figure 189).[274] When Montenegro resumed its sovereignty in 2006 – and indeed, slightly earlier – the Montenegrin eagle was changed to gold. It seems, although I cannot prove it, that this color change was a way of distinguishing the Montenegrin eagle

---

[271]   Later canonized as St. Petar of Cetinje.

[272]   A speculative image of Petar I's supposed arms can be seen on Wikimedia Commons at tinyurl.com/kvlz76l.

[273]   See his article "History of the Montenegrin Flag" on the Flags of the World website at tinyurl.com/lz69lsl. Prince Danilo's standard is shown in Figure 188.

[274]   Montenegro was the last of the Yugoslav "republics" to remain with Serbia within the rump former Yugoslavia. The breastshield places the golden lion on a plain red field, with no green compartment.

from that of Serbia. The Montenegrin double eagle is now officially gold with a lion heartshield; Figure 190 is the Montenegrin national flag in current use.[275]

DOUBLE EAGLE OUTLIERS

The use of the double eagle in the West has been concentrated in the lands discussed above. But there are outliers. For example, it has been estimated that 7% of the eagles in use in France in the earliest age of heraldry were bicephalic.[276] A classic French example is the seal of the Templar knight Guilliame de l'Aigle [William of the Eagle], from a seal of 1227 (Figure 191).[277] In the painting at left, the famous commander Bernard de Guesclin is being made Constable of France by King Charles V in 1370 – his arms, on his surcoat, are a black double eagle on white, beneath a red diagonal ribbon.[278]

There are English and Scottish examples of the double eagle used as a single supporter, usually by imperial concession. The Dukes of Marlborough had such a concession (John Churchill, the great commander and first Duke, was twice a Prince of the Holy Roman Empire); so did the family of Drummond-Murray of Mastrick.[279] The 17th century English poet John Milton bore for his arms a red double eagle on white.[280] The Scottish

---

275 In this design the heartshield again has a green compartment.

276 See Michel Pastoreau, *Traité d'Héraldique* [Treatise on Heraldry] (Paris, 1979), 149, citing Louis Bouly de Lesdain, "Les plus anciennes armoiries françaises [The oldest French arms] (1127-1300)," *Archives héraldiques suisses* [Swiss heraldic archives] (1897), 11:69-79, 94-103.

277 Several other 13th century French double-eagle seals are mentioned in Androudis (2013), note 9, at 215 n. 25.

278 *Argent, a double eagle sable, overall a riband gules.* The term *aigle eployée* was sometimes used in French to indicate a double eagle. Although the riband is shown on Guesclin's sleeve descending from the upper right, in ordinary use it descended from the upper left, as can just be discerned on his chest.

279 For an Internet image of the Marlborough arms, see "The Arms of Sir Francis Drake, Part 3" on the Wyverngules website at tinyurl.com/khz449k. For a fine modern rendition of the Drummond-Murray crowned eagle, granted to an ancestor by Charles V, see Brian North Lee, *Some Bookplates of Heralds and Related Ex-Libris* (London, 2003), 109.

280 See Anthony Wagner, *Historic Heraldry of Britain* (London, 1939), 90.

city of Perth has traditionally borne its arms on a double eagle (see Figure 192). The arms of Lanark include a double eagle on the shield rather than as a supporter; the double eagle cap badge of the former Lanarkshire Yeomanry regiment was derived from these arms. The former 1st King's Dragoon Guards had for their cap badge the double eagle of Austria, complete with the Austrian genealogical arms (see pages 51-52) on a breast-shield. This honored Emperor Franz Josef, who was Colonel-in-Chief of the regiment from 1895 until World War I.[281]

Both these British regiments have since been merged out of existence, but the Mercian Regiment survives (2014). Its double eagle cap badge is derived from the supposed arms of Leofric, the 11th century Earl of Mercia who is remembered by association with the legend of Lady Godiva. Leofric lived in pre-heraldic times, so these *attributed arms* are unhistorical, as are arms assigned by fanciful heraldic writers to such other historical and legendary characters as King David, Prince Hector of Troy, Alexander the Great, Judas Maccabaeus, Charlemagne, and many others including Death (a skull), Satan (frogs), Jesus Christ (instruments of the Passion), and God (the "Shield of the Trinity" diagram).[282] I mention this here because the double eagle was a favorite device for arms attributed to pre-heraldic persons, especially the knights of the Round Table (Mordred, Lot, Gawain).[283]

Julius Caesar (one of the "Nine Worthies" whose attributed arms are often shown in the front portions of medieval and Renaissance armorials), was also said to have borne a double eagle. (Above: "The Three Good Pagans," Hector, Alexander and Caesar, by Hans Burgkmair the Elder (1519)).[284] In Conrad Grünenberg's *Armorial* a page is

---

281 The Austrian eagle cap badge was discontinued in 1915 but reinstated in 1937. See T. J. Edwards, *Regimental Badges* (Aldershot, 1951), 61. For a good photographic image of the cap badge, see the British Northeast Medals website at <u>tinyurl.com/lajhtuu</u>.

282 For an interesting and well-illustrated treatment of the supposed arms of divine personalities, see Rodney Dennys, "The Heavenly Host in Heraldry," chapter 8 in his *The Heraldic Imagination* (New York, 1976), 89-112, and plates facing pp. 49 and 80.

283 For a facsimile of an Arthurian armorial see Lisa Jefferson, "Tournaments, Heraldry and the Knights of the Round Table," in James P. Carley and Felicity Ridley, eds., *Arthurian Literature XI* (Cambridge, 1996), 69 *ff.*

284 Note in the text figure by Burgkmair that the two necks of the double eagle cross, an extremely unusual posture. For an image of the notable mural of the Nine Worthies with their shields, in the Castle of Manta, Italy, attributed to Giacomo Jaquerio (early 15th century) and downloadable via

(footnote continues →)

devoted to the imagined arms of Roman emperors such as Tiberius and Vespasian, most of them variations of a double-eagle theme.[285]

There are other outliers. Figure 193 is a Danish seal from around 1600 – although the double eagle was established by this time as an imperial emblem in Germany, Denmark was never part of the Empire.[286] Figure 194 is a 1658 coin of Mihnea III (Michael Radu), Prince of Wallachia in what is now Romania. Figure 198 is a Hungarian closure fitting for a cloak, from the 13th century, an outstanding example of Romanesque gold work. A 1712 charter of the Georgian King Vakhtang VI, headed by a crowned double eagle in gold, is now in the Armenian National Archives in Tbilisi.[287]

In 1806 a double-eagle flag was created for the Russian-American Company, which administered the Russian colony in Alaska until the United States bought the territory in 1867. Figure 195 is the flag of the Company – a double eagle in the early 19th century style on a Russian national tricolor. The Company's flag also flew over its settlements in California.[288]

A further outlier is the Masonic double eagle, used as an emblem by the Scottish Rite (not actually Scottish at all, but the dominant Masonic organization in the United States).

(footnote continues …)

Wikigallery, see tinyurl.com/lecfep7. I think it is probable that the status of Caesar as the supposed "first of the Roman emperors" (although he was of course no such thing) led to the double eagle being attributed to him. Tsar Ivan IV (the Terrible) of Russia imagined he was literally descended from Julius Caesar, and that he bore a double eagle in his arms by inheritance from him. This is not historically possible, although an elaborate genealogy was prepared in Russia in later years to show that it was. There were also nine *female* worthies, including Penthesilea, Queen of the Amazons, also often shown with imagined shields of arms.

The portraits are imaginary. Contemporary portrait sculpture presents Caesar as bald, and Alexander's coins show him clean-shaven. Although Hector was of course fictional, or at least legendary, not even in Homer's imagination is he likely to have worn the long goatee of a Renaissance nobleman – Achilles would have grabbed right onto it.

[285]   Grünenberg, note 59, at frame 00011.

[286]   The date of around 1600 is based on Sven Tito Achen, *Danmarks Kommunevåbener* [Arms of Danish municipalities) (Copenhagen, 1992), 95.

[287]   It can be seen on Wikimedia Commons at tinyurl.com/knrnkcv. Medieval Georgia was within the Byzantine cultural sphere.

[288]   There is some controversy about the exact design of this flag, few examples of which were ever made. See the discussion on the relevant Flags of the World website page at tinyurl.com/qb2t8gg. I have selected the version officially reported in 1835, which also appears at tinyurl.com/p8xarw6 on the website of the Fort Ross Conservancy, which now administers the historic site of the Russian outpost in Northern California.

See Figure 196. It is also used as an emblem of specific degrees within the Masonic structure. The explanations of this emblem in Masonic literature are chaotic, contradictory, self-referential and riddled with obvious historical errors.[289] It would be pointless to try to parse or reconcile these sources.

One possibly meaningful explanation is that the eagle is a reference to the constituting authority of a supposed high Masonic council, meeting in France in the 18th century, called the Council of Emperors of the East and West. Whether there is any truth to this story or not, the *belief* that it was true could account for the use of the symbol. Another, complementary possibility lies in the career of Estienne Morin (1717?-1771), a French trader in what later became Haiti, who was supposedly given (or assumed) the right to establish Masonic lodges in the New World but not the Old. Whatever the true origin of this Scottish Rite emblem, it is in widespread use and adorns Masonic buildings, regalia, letterheads, and the like, in the manner of a trademark.

To close this section I will cite one example of many that could have been chosen from outside the European cultural sphere. In southern India supposedly lived a fearsome two-headed bird called *Gandaberunda*, a manifestation of Narasimha, himself part man and part lion and an incarnation of Vishnu, one of the principal gods of the Hindu pantheon.[290] Gandaberunda was the dynastic symbol of the Woyedar Dynasty that ruled the Kingdom of Mysore for centuries until the abolition of princely India in 1947. Figure 197 is the Woyedar emblem in a relatively domesticated, Europeanized form, taken from a Mysore revenue stamp first printed in 1932. It is still the central charge in the arms of the modern Indian state of Karnataka.[291]

THE DOUBLE EAGLE AS A POPULAR IMAGE

The importance of the double eagle in so many places, as a royal and later as a national symbol as well as a focus of nationalism and loyalty, has kept this strange image prominent for centuries in the imagination, and in the collective unconscious, of people in many parts of Europe. Unsurprisingly, it has been an important feature not only in such incidents of sovereignty as coins, seals, flags, regalia and military uniforms, but also in civil arts and handicrafts in many media. Figures 198-230 include a small but representative selection of these objects, arranged roughly chronologically (some items

---

[289] For example: the double eagle was transmitted from the Sumerian civilization at Lagash through Akkad to the Crusaders, Charlemagne used the double eagle to denote the union of Germany and Rome, it was the personal emblem of Frederick the Great of Prussia, etc.

[290] Images of Gandaberunda are given in Hubert de Vries' article cited in note 6 above.

[291] See the example on Wikimedia Commons at <u>tinyurl.com/lq3jvy7</u>.

84

are not dated). For each one I show, I could have selected a dozen others. When we chart the career of the double eagle in the West, these unofficial uses, deep in the culture, seem at least as important as the official ones imposed from the top.

Figure 198: Golden jeweled cloak fitting (Hungarian, 13th century).

Figure 199: Floor tiles (French, 13th century).

Figure 200: Alchemical image from the *Buch der Heiligen Dreifaltigkeit* [Book of the Holy Trinity] (early 15th century).[292]

Figure 201: Silver reliquary, from Zara on the Adriatic (15th century).

Figure 202: Gothic cloister window from Basilica of Our Lady, Maastricht, the Netherlands (completed 1559).

Figure 203: *Quaternionhumpen* (1615).[293]

Figure 204: German glass bottle (1615).

Figure 205: Italian armor (detail).

Figure 206: Detail of a carved bureau belonging to Albrecht von Wallenstein.[294]

Figure 207: Iron weathervane from Cologne.

Figure 208: The hyacinth "La Bella."[295]

Figure 209: Tyrolean hanging cabinet (18th century).

Figure 210: Russian painted wooden panel (c. 1740).

---

[292] The symbolism here is not political. Alchemy was a complex study, combining the precursor to modern chemistry and metallurgy with metaphors about the integration of personality and purification of the soul. The image is concerned with the three "basic" elements: sulphur (the caustic agent), salt (the preservative agent) and mercury (the product of refinement). The double eagle illustrated the alchemical principle SALVE ET COAGULA – let the elements first be separated and then recombined.

[293] A glass beaker with a Quaternion eagle painted or enameled onto it.

[294] Wallenstein, an important imperial general in the Thirty Years' War, died in 1634.

[295] Among the Austrian crown jewels. This 416 carat hyacinth, a semiprecious red zircon, was bought by Emperor Leopold I from a Hungarian family in 1686. See Twining, note 159, 13-14.

THE ATTACK (HYÖKKÄYS), BY EETU ISTO (1899).[296]

---

[296]   In this painting the Russian double eagle attacks *Suomi-neito*, the Maiden of Finland. The painting is an allegory of the so-called February Manifesto of Tsar Nicholas II (1899), which intensified the Russification of Finland, at the time a part of the Russian Empire with the Tsar as Grand Duke.

Figure 211: Italian faïence pitcher (c.1770).

Figure 212: Spanish colonial book stand (Mexican).[297]

Figure 213: Metal grille from the church of Cayara, near Potosí, Bolivia.

Figure 214: Window in Zarazino Palace, Moscow (late 18th century).

Figure 215: German iron stove plate (1787).

Figure 216: Roof of St. Stephen's Cathedral, Vienna (1831).[298]

Figure 217: Silver belt clasp from Troyan in Bulgaria (19th century).

Figure 218: Russian lace.[299]

Figure 219: Russian silver watch case.

Figure 220: Hand mirror (Bulgarian? c.1900?)

Figure 221: Russian enamel egg (1910).

Figure 222: Hood ornament, Russo-Balt fire engine (1912).

Figure 223: Russian war loan poster (1916) (detail).

Figure 224: Austrian war loan poster (1917).

Figure 225: Brass candlestick with arms of Lübeck (c.1920).

Figure 226: Dust jacket, German edition of Jean Cocteau, *L'Aigle à Deux Têtes* [The double eagle], (Munich, 1963).

Figure 227: Stencil graffito (Austrian, 2005).[300]

---

[297] The source dates it to the 18th century. Maybe so. The tin painting of Our Lady of Guadalupe suggests a Mexican origin, anyway.

[298] The cypher F I stands for Emperor Francis I.

[299] For similar lace from Austria, see Alan Summerly Cole, "Lace," in *Encyclopaedia Britannica* (New York, 1911), vol. 16, plate facing p. 38.

[300] The eagle's heads have been turned into video cameras, to symbolize state surveillance.

Figure 228: *Der Doppeladler*, by Hans Crepaz.[301]

Figure 229: Greek AEK football emblem t-shirt (contemporary).[302]

Figure 230: Austrian cooking patch (contemporary).

The Meaning of the Double Eagle

What is the meaning of the eagle with two heads? People unfamiliar with the heraldic role of this monster shudder at the sight of it – it is certainly a weird and creepy image. Although birds and snakes and other creatures have been known to survive with two heads, these freaks of nature still inspire shock and horror. How did an eagle with two heads come to stand for three mighty empires, and many other dominions besides? What is really going on here?

The answer, of course, is that no one knows. The iconographic history traces uncertainly back through the Eastern Roman Empire to its Asian hinterland. But this begs the question – why was it there? And why did so unlikely an image spread? Was it just an appealing symmetry, or did it mean something, and if so what?

Janus, the two-headed god of Rome, had faces on both sides of his head. He was one of the oldest Roman gods, appearing often at the beginning of lists of the gods; his temple in Rome was made of wood, a sign that his cult was very old. Janus was the god of doors, which of course open both out and in. He was the god also of the new year – Janus could see the past behind him, and the future ahead. At right is an ancient Roman coin with his image, one of the most common on old Roman coins. It is certain that the founders of the New Rome in Byzantium know this usage of old Rome, but the double eagle did not appear in Byzantium for many centuries after its re-foundation as a Roman capital.

---

301   Note the Tyrolean hats on the eagle's heads, and the Austrian imperial crown (*Rudolfskrone*) in the foreground (see note 159).

302   The logo design is "retro." The sleeker contemporary design can be seen on Wikipedia at tinyurl.com/krem7hn.

Nevertheless the double eagle's ability to see everywhere around, not only forward and back but to the sides as well (and up and down – it could fly!), and by extension like Janus to see the past and the future, made it a powerful beast. Who would not want a magical ally like that? This image is similar in spirit to those heraldic scenes (often featuring an eagle, as in the arms of Transylvania, see Figure 88) where a sun and a moon appear in the sky together. The message is that the eagle (and the ruler whose emblem it is) dominates by day and by night – in short dominates at all times, and everywhere. The double eagle is open to the same interpretation.

There are more specific interpretations, too. The eagle rules east and west – that is, Old Rome and New Rome, the two halves of the Roman Empire divided by Diocletian. I know of no examples in the archaeological record of the double eagle's use in the immediate post-division period, but it could certainly have been adopted later with this meaning intended. In the Eastern Empire the Church was closely associated with the state, and so the double eagle has been seen as expressing an imperial claim to govern the spiritual as well as the temporal worlds, and as continuing the Church's claims in both worlds after the Empire itself had fallen. This had overtones in the West as well, where the emperors were in conflict with the Popes for centuries on this very point.

East and West, Past and Present, Roman and Outlander, Church and State, Land and Sea, Europe and Asia, Here and There (meaning Everywhere) – there are many inter-pretations.[303] But there is no documentation, and no definitive answer. Writings in explanation are either speculations, or unsupported assertions, or more or less blind copyings of the speculations and assertions of earlier writers. We would do better to accept that we will never know the true historical explanation for certain, but that all of them have *poetic* validity. And more besides – we can close this review with the motto of the mighty Emperor Charles V, borne beneath his double eagle: *Plus Ultra! More Beyond!*

---

[303]   One resonant one is the medieval concept that the King has two bodies – personal and institutional. See Ernst H. Kantorowicz, *The King's Two Bodies: A Study in Mediaeval Political Theology* (Princeton, 1957).

GALLERY OF ILLUSTRATIONS

Figure 1. Sumerian cylinder seal from Lagash.

Figure 2. Hittite cliff sculpture from Alaca Höyük.

Figure 3. Hittite seal impression from Boğazkale (18th century BC).

Figure 4. Ornament from Mycenae.

Figure 5. Coin from Amida (c. 1180).

Figure 6. Bas-relief from Amida (c. 1208).

Figure 7. Artuquid coin from Amida (1217).

Figure 8. Tile from Kubadabad Palace, Konya (early 13th century).

Figure 9. Carved image from Divriği Great Mosque.

Figure 10. Bas-relief from the walls of Konya (c. 1221).

Figure 11. Zengid coin (late 12th century).

Figure 12. Detail from Egyptian brass incense burner (c. 1278).

Figure 13. Egyptian ceramic dish (late 13th century).

Figure 14. Egyptian potsherd.

Figure 15. Egyptian potsherd.

Figure 16. Brocade from Palermo (before 1309).

Figure 17. Sculpted roundel from Palermo Cathedral (12th century).

Figure 18. Gold tari coin, Sicilian, (c. 1202).

Figure 19: Textile fragment from "Cloak of the Virgin," Thiur, France (12th century).

Figure 20. Silk fragment from tomb of St. Bernard Calvò, Vich, Spain (1071-1106).

Figure 21. Textile fragment from Islamic Spain (12th century).

Figure 22. Detail from "Shroud of St. Amadus" (12th century).

Figure 23. Bas-relief from church in Gensac-La-Pollue, France (12th century).

Figure 24. Tiles from Abbey Church of Vivoin, France (13th century).

Figure 25. Detail from a fresco in Clermont Cathedral, France (12th century).

Figure 26: Detail of church fresco from Asnières-sur-Vègre, France (12th century).

Figure 28. Illuminated initial from French manuscript (c. 1150).

Figure 29. Line drawing of an eagle detail, Shroud of St. Germanus, Auxerre, France.

Figure 30: Miniature of Sebastocrator Constantine Palaeologue and his wife Eirene (1310).

Figure 31: Locket of Princess Tamar (1294).

Figure 32: Relief in the Church of the Parigoritissa, Arta (c. 1295).

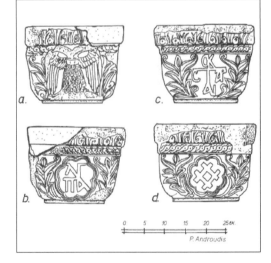

Figure 33. Marble slab from metropolitan church of Mistra (15th century).

Figure 34: Earring of Maria Palaeologina, Queen of Serbia (early 14th century).

Figure 35. Four faces of a capital in the Basilica of St. Demetrios, Thessalonika (first half of 14th century).

Figure 36: Byzantine double eagle with Palaeologue monogram.

Figure 37: Frecso of Manuel I of Trebizond, from Hagia Sophia of Trebizond (mid-13th century).

Figure 38. Gattilusi inscription, Chorea, Samothrace, 1433. Panels between inscriptions are: single eagle, tetragrammatic cross composition, double eagle, Palaeologue monogram.

Figure 39. Galley cabin of Emperor John VIII. Detail after Filarete bronze door (completed 1445).

Figure 40: Printer's mark of Zacarias Calliergi (Venice, 1499).

Figure 41. Byzantine banner embroidery (c. 1366-70).

Figure 42. Detail of head from Figure 41.

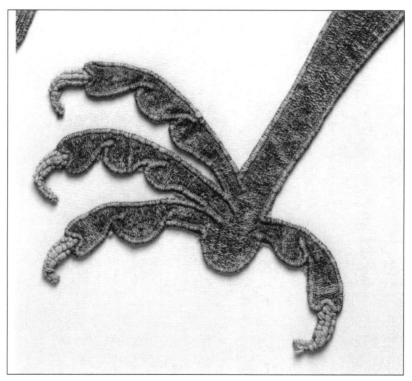

Figure 43. Detail of foot from Figure 41.

Figure 44. Brooch of Gisela of Swabia (10th century).

Figure 45. Silver penny of Leopold V of Austria (1197).

Figure 46: Wall tile from Abbey Church of St. Emmeram, Regensburg (mid-12th century).

Figure 47: Seal of Count Ludwig von Sarwarden (c. 1185).

Figure 48: Seal of Poppo, Count of Henneberg (c. 1212).

Figure 49. Seal of Heinrich von Kirkel (1230).

Figure 50. Supposed arms of Emperor Frederick II, from Matthew Paris' *Historia Anglorum* (c. 1258; image inverted).

Figure 51: Gold *augustalis* of Frederick II (first half of 13th century).

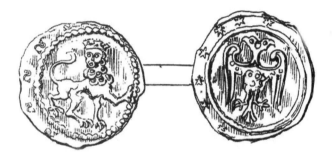

Figure 52: Coin of Otto IV (reigned 1198-1218).

Figure 53. Seal of the infant Wenceslaus IV, King of Bohemia (1363).

Figure 54: Imperial seal of Sigismund (cut in 1417; first used 1434).

Figure 55. Seal of City of Friedberg (1260).

Figure 56. Seal of City of Friedberg (1344).

Figure 57: Seal of City of Kaiserswerd (13th century).

Figure 58. City banner of Cologne (c. 1500).

Figure 59. Seal of the Jewish community in Augsburg, Germany (1298).

Figure 60. Thalers of imperial cities during the reign of Charles V.

Figure 61. Imperial banner, by Jacob Kallenberg (1545).

Figure 62. Lübeck boundary marker (contemporary).

Figure 63. Imperial crown (so-called Crown of Charlemagne).

Figure 65. Emperor Sigismund at the Council of Constance, from Ulrich von Richenthal's *Chronik* (1483).

Figure 64. Crown of Emperor Frederick III, from his tomb (1493).

Figure 66. Silver coin of Margaret of Constantinople (Flemish, 1244).

Figure 67. Triple eagle page from *Grünenberg's Armorial* (1483).

Figure 68. Gold coin of Charles V.

Figure 69. From licensing page, *Ad Carolum V Panegyricus* (c. 1536?).

Figure 70: From dedication page, *Conquista del Peru* (1535).

Figure 71: Arms from imperial edict (1550).

Figure 72. Woodcut by Heinrich Vogtherr the Elder, c. 1547-48.

Figure 74: Arms of Academia Boyacense de Historia. Tunja, Colombia.

Figure 73. City gate of Toledo, Spain.

Figure 75: Double eagle and snake, from the mission church in Querétaro, Mexico.

Figure 76: Mystical Arms of Spain, from Juan de Caramuel y Lobkowitz,
***Declaración Mystica de las Armas de España* (Brussels, 1636).**

Figure 77. Flag of the Austrian Netherlands
(red, white, yellow).

Figure 78. Seal of Engelbert
Ludick van Dijck (1318).

Figure 79. Arms of the Margraves of
Antwerp (1500).

Figure 80. Arms of Johan Lodewijk van
Elderen, Prince-Bishop of Liège (1691).

Figure 81. Modern city flag of Arnhem,
Netherlands (blue and white).

108

Figure 82. Small arms of Austrian Empire, by Hugo Gerard Ströhl (1900).

Figure 83. Elaborated version of Austrian genealogical arms, by Emil Doepler the Younger (1880).

Figure 84. Full arms of Austria, by Agi Lindegren (1899).

110

Figure 85. Coronation medal of
Ferdinand I (1558).

Figure 86. Great seal of Leopold I for
Transylvania (1696).

Figure 87. Eagle of the *Hoch- und
Deutschmeister* (Francis I, ruled 1745-65).

Figure 88. Transylvanian ducat of
Maria Theresa (1777).

Figure 89. Imperial great arms of 1915, by Hugo Gerard Ströhl.

Figure 90. Maria Theresa thaler (reverse).

Figure 91: Colour of an imperial cuirassier regiment (c. 1700) (black on red).

Figure 92. Colour of a Hungarian heiduck regiment (c. 1700) (red and green).

Figure 93. Colour of imperial Baden-Durlach infantry regiment (black, yellow, red).

Figure 94: Regimental flag of Austrian Walloon regiment (late 18th century) (yellow field; border in yellow, white, red and black).

Figure 95: Schützkompanie Tramin colour (1779 pattern) (dark green and white).

Figure 96: Austrian infantry colour of Empress Maria Theresa (black on gold).

Figure 97: Ensign of Imperial Austrian Navy (black and gold).

Figure 98. German Confederation war flag (black eagle on gold; black, red and gold stripes).

Figure 99: Small arms of German Principality of Schwarzburg-Rudolstadt (1899).

Figure 100: Austrian army belt buckle.

Figure 101: Badge of the Austrian Order of the Iron Crown.

Figure 102: Arms of (Austrian) Kingdom of Lombardy-Venetia.

Figure 103: Austro-Hungarian imperial standard (1894 pattern).

Figure 104: Title page of sheet music for Josef Franz Wagner, *Unter dem Doppeladler Marsch* **(1893; detail).**

Figure 105: *Militärmark* of the
Austrian 11th Dragoons.

**Figure 106: Art deco design by Koloman
Moser.**

**Figure 107: Emblem of the imperial
Austrian Red Cross Society.**

**Figure 108: Officials' rank flag of
the Austrian Federal State (1936)
(red and white).**

Figure 109: Emblem of Vienna (1934-38).

**Figure 110: Arms of Fiume, by
Hugo Gerard Ströhl (1900).**

Figure 111. Armorial coin of Pope
Alexander VIII (Ottoboni) (1589).

Figure 112. Arms of Garganelli.

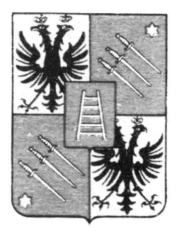

Figure 113: Arms of Seregi
di Cortesia.

Figure 114: Arms of Filangeri.

Figure 115: Arms of
Commune of Velletri.

Figure 116: Seal of Philip of Savoy
(c. 1278).

Figure 117: Gold *scudo* of William IX of Montferrat (ruled 1494-1518).

Figure 118: Palio banner (*contrada d'Aquila*) (black on gold).

Figure 119: Eagle at the Ecumenical Patriarchate in Istanbul.

Figure 120: Flag of the Greek Orthodox Church.

Figure 121: Emblem of the Greek Orthodox Church of Australia.

Figure 122: Greek Red Cross decoration (1956).

Figure 123: Postage stamp of the Northern Epirus Republic (1914).

Figure 124: Coin of Cyprus under the presidency of Archbishop Makarios (1974).

Figure 125: Seal of the self-styled "House of Lascaris Comnenus of Constantinople."

Figure 126: Seal of Grand Prince Ivan III (1497).

Figure 127: Silver *denge* of Mikhail Borisovich, Prince of Tver (before 1486).

Figure 128: Coin attributed to Jani Beg, khan of the Golden Horde (c. 1350).

Figure 129: Ruble coin (1707).   **Figure 130: Five kopek coin (1833).**   **Figure 131: Five kopek coin (1858).**

Figure 132: Page from Slavonic Bible (1663).

Figure 133: *Jeton* of graduates of the Moscow Technical School (19th century).

119

Figure 134: Badge, Russian Order of St. Andrew First-Called.

Figure 135: Helmet of the Russian Life Guards Regiment.

Figure 136: Arms of Chudovo (1899).

Figure 137: Colour-staff finial from a Russian Guards Regiment.

Figure 138: Russian military guidon (17th century).

Figure 139: Colour of the Ryazan Carabineer Regiment (1763).

Figure 140: Colonel's colour, Guards Artillery Train and Bombardier Company.

Figure 141: Russian line infantry regimental colour (standard 1803 pattern).

Figure 142. Flag of an imperial Russian envoy or resident (1896 pattern) (stripes white-red-blue).

Figure 143: Imperial standard for use afloat (1858 pattern).

Figure 144: Seal of the Russian Provisional Government (1917).

Figure 145: Russian state standard (19th century).

Figure 146: Arms of Russian Federation (1993 pattern).

Figure 147: Ruble coin (2014).

Figure 148: Russian Presidential standard (1994 pattern).

Figure 149: Flag of "Donetsk People's Republic" (2014) (stripes black-red-blue).

Figure 150: Seal of Skanderbeg.

Figure 151: Supposed arms of Skanderbeg.

Figure 152: Flag of the Principality of Albania (1914).

Figure 154: Standard of Prince Vili I (Wilhelm of Wied).

Figure 155: Albanian national flag (1992 pattern).

RUBEA
VEXILLA
NIGRIS ET
BICIPITIBUS
DISTINCTA
AQUILIS GEREBAT
SCANDERBECUS

DANS SES
ESTENDARS
QUI
ESTOIENT
TOUS ROUGES
SCANDERBEG
PORTOIT UNE
AIGLE NOIRE
A DEUX TESTES

Barletius:
Historia de
vita et gestis
Scanderbegi.
Romae. 1506.
FOLIO. XV.

Lavardin:
Histoire de
Scanderbeg,
roy d'Albanie.
Paris. 1576.
PAGE 42.

Figure 153: Historical design by Charles F. B. Morse (1911).

Figure 156: Albanian national arms (1992 pattern).

Figure 157: Albanian revenue stamp (1920).

Figure 158: Albanian gold coin (1927).

Figure 159: Flag image for Serbia from the map of Angelino Dulcert (1339).

Figure 160: Ring of Queen Teodora (mid-14th century).

Figure 161: Fresco of Prince Miroslav in Byzantine-style robe, Bijelo Polje, Montenegro.

125

Figure 162: Metal roundel from a chandelier in the Markov monastery, Skopje (c. 1366).

Figure 163: Coin of Bulgarian Emperor Michael Shishman (1327).

Figure 164: Arms of Nemanjić from the Korenić-Neorić Armorial (1595).

Figure 165: Arms of Stefan Lazarević by Ulrich von Richenthal (1483).

Figure 167. Arms of Serbia from the *Stematografija* (1741).

Figure 168: Seal of Karageorge.

Figure 169: Serbian royal arms (1899).

Figure 170: Serbian state flag (1882 pattern) (stripes red-blue-white).

Figure 171: Arms of Obrenović Dynasty.

Figure 172: Arms of King Stephan Lazarović as a Knight of the Dragon.

Figure 173: Yugoslav royal arms (c. 1922).

127

Figure 174: Arms of Yugoslav Kingdom (below) and Yugoslav royal arms (c. 1933).

Figure 175: Yugoslav royal standard (1937 pattern). Dark red background, red-white-blue border.

Figure 176: Serbian Order of the White Eagle.

Figure 177: Arms of State Union of Serbia and Montenegro (2006).

Figure 178: Serbian national flag (2009 pattern).

Figure 179: Serbian presidential standard (2009 pattern).

Figure 180: Colour of the Serbian Air Force (reverse) (2010).

Figure 181. City flag of Leskovac, Serbia.

Figure 182: *Graffito* **from a Vienna park (c. 1992).**

Figure 183: Heading page of the *Oktoih Prvoglasnik* (1494).

Figure 184: Montenegrin Military Bravery Medal (1841).

Figure 185: Arms of Montenegro (1899).

Figure 186: Montenegrin gold 100-perper coin (1910).

Figure 187: Montenegrin flag (19th century).

Figure 188: Standard of Prince Danilo I (1852).

Figure 189: Arms of Montenegro (1993).

Figure 190: Montenegrin national flag (2004 pattern).

Figure 191: Seal of Guilliame de l'Aigle (1278).

Figure 192: Arms of Perth, Scotland.

Figure 193: Danish local seal.

Figure 194: Copper shilling of Mihnea III (Michael Radu), Prince of Wallachia (1658).

Figure 195: Flag of the Russian-American Company (1835).

Figure 196: Emblem of 33° Mason, Scottish Rite.

Figure 197: Mysore revenue stamp (1932; detail).

Figure 198: Golden jeweled cloak fitting (Hungarian, 13th century).

Figure 199: French floor tiles (13th century).

Figure 201: Reliquary from Zara (15th century).

Figure 200: Alchemical image from the *Buch der Heiligen Dreifaltigkeit* [Book of the Holy Trinity) (early 15th century).

Figure 202: Gothic cloister window from Basilica of Our Lady, Maastricht, Netherlands (1559).

Figure 203: *Quaternionhumpen* (1615).

133

Figure 204: German glass bottle (1615).

Figure 205: Italian armor (detail).

Figure 206: Wallenstein's carved bureau (detail).

Figure 207: Weathervane from Cologne.

Figure 208: Hyacinth "La Bella."

Figure 209: Tyrolean hanging cabinet (18th century).

Figure 210: Russian painted wood panel (c. 1740).

Figure 211: Italian faïence pitcher (c. 1770) (detail).

Figure 212: Spanish colonial book stand (Mexican).

Figure 213: Metal grille from Heart of Jesus chapel, church of Cayara, near Potosí, Bolivia.

135

Figure 214: Window from Zazarino Palace, Moscow (late 18th century).

Figure 215: German iron stove plate (1787).

Figure 216: Roof of St. Stephen's Cathedral, Vienna (1831).

Figure 217: Silver belt clasp from Troyan, Bulgaria (late 19th century).

Figure 218: Russian lace.

Figure 219: Russian watch case.

Figure 220: Brass hand mirror (Bulgarian? c.1900?).

Figure 221: Russian enameled egg (1910).

Figure 222: Hood ornament, Russo-Balt fire engine (1912).

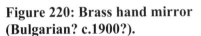

Figure 223: Russian war loan poster (1916) (detail).

Figure 224: Austrian war loan poster (1917).

Figure 225: Brass candlestick with arms of Lübeck (c.1920).

Figure 226: Dust jacket from 1963 German edition of Jean Cocteau's *L'Aigle à Deux Têtes*.

Figure 227: Stencil graffito (Austrian, 2005).

Figure 228: *Der Doppeladler*, by Hans Crepaz.

Figure 229: Greek AEK football emblem T-shirt (contemporary).

Figure 230: Austrian cooking patch (contemporary).

SOURCES OF THE ILLUSTRATIONS

Citations to *line numbers* refer to the numbered entries in this section.
Citations to *notes* refer to footnotes in the main text.

COVERS

1. **Front cover: Russian eagle.** From the *Imperial Book of Titles* (Tsarskiye Titulyarnik, Царский Титулярник) (1672). Image from Wikimedia Commons at <u>tinyurl.com/mahapw6</u> (see note 205, page 64 above).

2. **Inside front cover: Austrian Empire middle arms.** From Hugo Gerard Ströhl, *Oesterreichisch-Ungarische Wappenrolle* [Austro-Hungarian armorial] (Vienna, 1900; modern reprint, Schleinbach [Austria], 2010), plate 4. Image downloadable on Wikimedia Commons at <u>tinyurl.com/kh6x94k</u>. For a gallery of expandable and downloadable images from this work, in color, see the Estonian hot.ee website at <u>tinyurl.com/pqztqzs</u>.

3. **Inside back cover: Middle Arms of Russian Empire.** From the official United States Navy flag book *Flags of Maritime Nations* (Washington, 1899), 53.

4. **Back cover: Quaternion Eagle.** *Das Hailig Romisch Reich mit Sampt seinen Gelidern* [The Holy Roman Empire with all its members], by Hans Burgkmair the Elder, c 1510. Image from Wikimedia Common at <u>tinyurl.com/ku4m7r6</u>. David de Negker, mentioned in the Wikimedia title, was the publisher but not the artist.

FOREMATTER

5. **Title page. Arms of the Holy Roman Empire.** From Peterman Etterlyn, *Chronique Suisse* [Swiss chronicle] (Basel, 1507); image after Etterlyn by Brother Fidèle-Gabriel [Paul-Gabriël Dufour] for Émile Gevaert, *L'Héraldique: Son Ésprit, Son Langage, les Applications* [Heraldry: Its spirit, language and applications] (Brussels, 1923), 47, fig. 71.

6. **Table of Contents tailpiece.** Heraldic ornament by Agi [August] Lindegren, from Fredrik-Ulrik von Wrangel, *Les Maisons Souveraines de l'Europe* [Sovereign houses of Europe] (Stockholm 1898-99), 1:40.

7. **Dedication. Portrait of Whitney Smith.** Photograph by Austin Smith, reprinted with permission.

8. **Frontispiece. *Collegium Poetarum.*** Woodcut by Hans Burgkmair the Elder (1510), reproduced from Hubert Schrade, *Sinnbilder des Reiches* [Symbols of the *Reich*] (Munich, 1938), fig. 25. This work is a rich source of German double-eagle images.

9. **Preface vignette.** Arms of Plaue an der Havel, Germany. By Otto Hupp, from *Die Ortswappen des Königreichs Preussen* [Local arms of the Kingdom of Prussia] (Bremen, 1914). Image from the Dutch civic heraldry website Heraldry of the World at www.ngl.nl.

10. **Preface tailpiece.** Coin of Frederick III (emperor 1452-93). From Heinrich Philipp Cappe, *Die Münzen der deutschen Kaiser und Könige des Mittelalters* [The coins of the German emperors and kings of the Middle Ages] (Dresden, 1848), part I, plate 16, no. 271, illustrating 1:182, no. 836.

11. **Author's note vignette.** Seal of German noble family of Bülow (1299), from Friedrich Crull, "Die Wappen der bis 1360 in den Heutigen Grenzen Meklenburgs" [Arms before 1360 within the present borders of Mecklenberg] in *Jahrbüch des Vereins für Mecklenburgische Geschichte und Altertumskunde* [Yearbook of the society of Mecklenburg history and archaeology] (Schwerin, 1887), 52:34, 50, digitized by Dokumentenserver der Landes-bibliothek Mecklenburg-Vorpommern [Document server of the Mecklenburg-Western Pomerania state library] at tinyurl.com/lwwjh36.

12. **Author's note tailpiece.** Image from the *Wappenbuch des Hans Ulrich Fisch* [Armorial of Hans Ulrich Fisch] (Aarau, 1627), 47r, from the digitized facsimile on the website of the Staatsarchiv Aargau [State Archive of Aargau Canton, Switzerland] at tinyurl.com/o3pu6lt. This armorial manuscript was created in an attempt to show a genealogical relationship between the Fisch family and the House of Habsburg, whose original seat was at Habsburg Castle in Aargau Canton. The armorial has many superb double eagle paintings.

13. **Map showing diffusion of the double eagle image in Europe.** By the author, drawn on a blank map from the website of St. Margaret's School, Tappahannock, Virginia, at tinyurl.com/mwyuucj. Redrawn by Charles Waltmire.

TEXT FIGURES

14. **Page 15: Imperial herald.** Line drawing by Ignacio Vicente Cascante, from his *Heráldica General y Fuentes de las Armas de España* [General heraldry and sources of the arms of Spain] (Barcelona, 1956), 105. Vicente Cascante appears to have drawn it after the illustration in Hugo Gerard Ströhl, *Heraldischer Atlas* [Heraldic atlas] (Stuttgart, 1899), plate 1, fig. 9. Ströhl himself attributed the image to a 16th century woodcut by Michael Ostendorfer (d. 1559), showing the imperial herald Kaspar Sturm. A digitization of Ströhl's classic book appears on the Austria-Forum website at tinyurl.com/jvtckha.

15. **Page 22: Attack on Constantinople by the Crusaders, 1204.** From a miniature by an unknown artist, in an edition of Geoffroi de Villehardouin, *De la Conquête de Constantinople* [On the conquest of Constantinople] published in Venice around 1330. Image from Wikimedia Commons at tinyurl.com/o49y5dq.

16. **Page 23: Flag of the emperor of Constantinople.** From *El Libro del conoscimiento de todos los reinos* [Book of knowledge of all the kingdoms], an anonymous manuscript of the last quarter of the 14th century, published by the Hakluyt Society as Clements Markham, ed., *Book of the Knowledge...*, Second Series, No. 29 (London, 1912). The image is from Plate 17, no 82. See note 42 on page 24 above.

17. **Page 23: Coin of co-emperors John V and Matthew Cantacuzene (c. 1450).** Image from Wikimedia Commons at tinyurl.com/qdfqjc3. Attribution: Classical Numismatic Group, Inc. http://www.cngcoins.com.

18. **Page 25: Coin of Emperor Manuel II.** Image from the expandable "Browsing Byzantine Empire Coinage of Manuel II" gallery on the Wildwinds coin website at tinyurl.com/qclqoen.

19. **Page 28: Journey to Italy of Emperor John VIII.** By Filarete, from the bronze doors of Old St. Peter's Basilica, Rome (completed 1445). Image reproduced from "The Winter Voyage Going Over," posted November 14, 2010 on the Surprised by Time website at tinyurl.com/nx6nje7. The posting contains a translation of the account of the Emperor's 1437 journey to Italy recorded by Sylvestros Syropoulos (c. 1400 - c. 1453) in his *Memoirs*; see also http://syropoulos.co.uk/translation.htm. The image is the best I could find despite its low resolution; apparently truncated in the source, it enlarges there with a click. For a line drawing of the double-eagle segment, see Figure 39.

20. **Page 29: Fresco from Gozzo Castle, Austria.** Photograph by Richard Cieslar, reproduced from the Austrian Meinbezirk website at tinyurl.com/maljpyz. For a different view of the fresco, see *ibid.* at tinyurl.com/mnq9lhu.

21. **Page 32: Map of Holy Roman Empire.** Detail of map from the University of Calgary's Applied History Group, reproduced from the Netserf academic resource website at tinyurl.com/m76zlpp. The link to the Calgary website has since become inoperative.

22. **Page 33: Portrait of Emperor Frederick II.** Engraving from an architectural medallion in the church of Porto Santo in Andria (Apulia), Italy. Published as Illustration 2 in Marjorie Bowen, *Sundry Great Gentlemen: Some Essays in Historical Biography* (London, 1928). The complete book is available electronically from Project Gutenberg of Australia at tinyurl.com/mc4phdf.

23. **Page 36: Portrait of Emperor Sigismund.** Attributed to Pisanello. The original is in the Kunsthistorischesmuseum [Art history museum], Vienna. Image from Wikimedia Commons at tinyurl.com/l5uxh2y.

24. **Page 38: Emperor Frederick VI, from the *Grosse Heidelberger Liederhandschrift*** [Great Heidelberg song manuscript]. Page 6r in the *Codex Manesse*. Image from Wikimedia Commons, at tinyurl.com/jwl7qzp. The entire *Codex Manesse*, the principal (but not the only) manuscript of the *Liederhandschrift*, has been digitized on the University of Heidelberg's website; this image appears there at tinyurl.com/l2bdnpl.

25. **Page 43: Tomb sculpture of King Ottokar II of Bohemia (c. 1377).** The tomb, by Peter Parler, is in the Cathedral of St. Vitus in Prague. The line drawing is from Josef Novak, *Štátne Znaky v Čechách a na Slovensku Dnes aj v Minulosti* [National emblems in the Czech Republic and Slovakia today and in the past] (Bratislava, 1990), 31.

26. **Page 46: Portrait of Emperor Charles V.** Detail of *Portrait of Charles V Seated*, by Titian (1548), in the Alte Pinakothek (Old picture gallery), Munich. Some dispute the attribution to Titian and believe it was painted by Lambert Sustris. Image from Wikimedia Commons at tinyurl.com/lehggxx.

27. **Page 51. Portrait of Empress Maria Theresa.** From a modern restrike of the 1780 Maria Theresa thaler, on the iCollector auction site at tinyurl.com/n898431. This is the obverse of the coin shown in Figure 90.

28. **Page 54. Portrait of Emperor Francis Joseph I.** By Ludwig Michalek (1859-1942); charcoal on canvas, c. 1915. Image from the Trieste Daily Blogspot website entry for February 16, 2012, at tinyurl.com/l9dqlyh.

29. **Page 58. *Die Widerpringung Maylannd zum Reich*** [The restoration of Milan to the Empire]. By Albrecht Altdorfer the Elder. In the Albertina Museum, Vienna; image from Wikimedia Commons at tinyurl.com/lff2ez7.

30. **Page 62. Monk waving Orthodox flag.** Photograph by Stella Tsolakidou, from "The Monk Who Waves at Planes," posted April 20, 2013 on the Greek Reporter website at tinyurl.com/nmbr9sa.

31. **Page 63. Greek military ceremony.** Photograph from a November 4, 2011 posting on the Greek National Pride website, at tinyurl.com/lotq2xe.

32. **Page 64. Portrait of Grand Prince Ivan III.** From Wikimedia Commons at tinyurl.com/prptea8, reproducing an image from the *Tsarskiye Titulyarnik* (1672). See note 205.

33. **Page 67. Herald of the Order of the White Eagle.** Designed by A. Sharleman; painting by Boris Kene. In the Russian State Historical Archives; reprinted in V. A. and D. V. Durov, *Russian State Symbolics* (Moscow 2003), 195.

34. **Page 69. Portrait of Boris Yeltsin.** Unidentified newspaper image.

35. **Page 70. Portrait of Skanderbeg.** Detail from a larger portrait, part of the Prosopa project of Panagiota Kouvari and "Gigas." Their work can be seen at the Prosopa website at prosopa.eu.

36. **Page 72. National Assembly at Vlorë (1912).** From Jaho Brahaj, *Flamuri i Kombit Shqiptar* [Flag of the Albanian nation] (Tiranë, 2002), 161.

37. **Page 76. Portrait of Milan I (Obrenović), King of Serbia.** Image by an unknown photographer, from Wikimedia Commons at tinyurl.com/m93twcv, citing Felix Philipp Kanitz, *Das Königreich Serbien und das Serbenvolk* [The Kingdom of Serbia and the Serbian people] (Leipzig, 1914), 230, digitized on the Open Library website at tinyurl.com/ol9mpfm.

38. **Page 77: Serbian battle flags from World War I.** Image from Wikimedia Commons at tinyurl.com/lwb29vx. Photographed at the Military Museum, Belgrade.

39. **Page 80: Portrait of Prince Danilo I of Montenegro.** Artist unknown; image from Wikimedia Commons at tinyurl.com/q964k9x.

40. **Page 81. Bernard de Guesclin made Constable of France.** This painting is credited in Internet sources as belonging to the British Library, but their Manuscripts Reference Service is unable to identify it. It has the look of a 15th century French miniature. Image from Spanish Wikipedia at tinyurl.com/nn65dm6.

41. **Page 82. *The Three Good Pagans.*** By Hans Burgkmair the Elder (1519), in the Kupferstich-Kabinett, Staatliche Kunst-Sammlungen [Copper-engravings cabinet, state art collection], Dresden.

42. **Page 86. *The Attack.*** Painting by Eetu Isto (1899) in the National Museum of Finland, Helsinki. Image from Wikimedia Commons at tinyurl.com/qy6vv8l.

43. **Page 88. Roman coin with head of Janus.** A two-as copper coin, illustrated in Oskar Seyffert *et al.*, *A Dictionary of Classical Antiquities* (New York, 1899). Image from Minerva Classics website at tinyurl.com/kncwogt. The work, which appeared in many editions, was originally published in London, without a date, but before 1879.

44. **Page 89. Tailpiece to the main text.** Austrian imperial herald. This image appears in Vicente Cascante's *Heráldica General*, line 14, alongside the one mentioned in line 5. Like the other, it follows an illustration by Hugo Gerard Ströhl in his *Heraldischer Atlas*, line 14, plate 2, this time Figure 4. Ströhl attributed the image to a pen-and-ink drawing by Hans Holbein (the Younger?) in the Staatliche Kunst-Sammlungen [State art collection], Dresden.

45. **Page 139. Headpiece to Sources of the Illustrations.** From Khristofor Žefarović *et al.*, ed., *Izobraženij Oružij Iliričeskih Stematografija* (Novi Sad, 1961), 19. This work is a facsimile of the original printed book from 1741.

46. **Page 159. Tailpiece to Sources of the Illustrations.** Byzantine stone slab from Beroe (Stara Zagora), Bulgaria. By Pascal Androudis, from his "Les premières apparitions attestées de l'aigle bicéphale dans l'art roman d'Occident (XIe-XIIe siècles): Origines et symbolique" [The first appearances of the two-headed eagle in the Romanesque art of the West (11th-12th centuries): Origins and symbolism], *Nis and Byzantium* (Niš, Serbia, 2013), 11:210. See note 28.

47. **Page 160. Tailpiece to the Colophon.** Postage stamp (Scott No. 53) issued by the Albanian Control Commission at Korçë in eastern Albania during unsettled conditions in 1914. Image from the Albania page of the StampMasterAlbum website at tinyurl.com/mfx9mbr.

48. **Page 160. Portrait of the author.** By Klaudia Nelson.

GALLERY FIGURES

49. **Figure 1: Cylinder seal from Lagash.** From Alexander Soloviev, "Les emblèmes héraldiques de Byzance et des Slaves" [Heraldic emblems of Byzantium and of the Slavs], Seminarium Kondakovianum (Prague, 1935), 7:123, fig. 1.

50. **Figure 2: Cliff sculpture from Alaca Höyük [Eyük], Turkey.** From Georges Perrot and Charles Chipiez, *Histoire de l'Art dans l'Antiquité* (Paris, 1882-88), vol. 4, fig. 343, reprinted in Eugène-Félicien-Albert Goblet, Count d'Alviella, *The Migration of Symbols* (Westminster, 1894; modern reprint New York, 1956), 21.

51. **Figure 3: Seal impression from Boğazkale [Bogazköy], Turkey (18th century BC).** In the Museum of Anatolian Civilizations, Ankara; image from "Meluhha Metallurgy and Hieroglyphs: Socio-Cultural Context" on the Bharatkalyan97 website at tinyurl.com/k7uh22k.

52. **Figure 4: Ornament from Mycenae.** From Heinrich Schliemann, *Mykenae* (Leipzig, 1878), 213, fig. 276; digitzed on the University of Heidelberg website at tinyurl.com/n32mw97.

53. **Figure 5: Coin from Amida (c. 1180).** From Soloviev (1935), line 49, 125, fig. 5.

54. **Figure 6: Bas-relief from Amida (c. 1208).** *Id.*, 124, fig. 4. Image reproduced in Hubert de Vries' article "Two-Headed Eagle," on his Hubert-Herald website at tinyurl.com/kqezyhk, crediting Max van Berchem *et al.*, *Amida* (Heidelberg, 1910).

55. **Figure 7. Coin of Artuquid ruler Al-Malik as-Salih Nasir as-Din Mahmud of Amida (1217).** Line drawing by Fidèle-Gabriel in Gevaert, line 5, 43, fig. 65(b).

56. **Figure 8: Tile from Kubadabad Palace, Konya (early 13th century).** Image from the website of the Karatay Museum of Seljuk Ceramics, Konya, at tinyurl.com/mfjw6kg.

57. **Figure 9. Carved image from Divriği Great Mosque, Turkey (c. 1229).** Image from Spanish Wikipedia at tinyurl.com/mzsak7p.

58. **Figure 10: Bas-relief from walls of Konya (c. 1221).** From De Vries, line 54. A better image appears on the Studyblue website at tinyurl.com/jw76kjr (captions unblur on highlighting).

59. **Figure 11. Zengid coin (late 12th century).** It is a dirham of Imad al-din Zengi. Published in de Vries, line 54, crediting Ludwig A. Clericus, "Zur Urgeschichte des Doppeladlers" [On the early history of the double eagle] in *Vierteljahrsschrift für Heraldik, Sphragistik und Genealogie* [Quarterly of heraldry, sphragistics and genealogy] (Berlin, 1875), vol. 3. Image from Russian VGD Genealogical Forum web page at tinyurl.com/m8duh8o.

60. **Figure 12: Detail of Egyptian brass incense burner (Mamluke, c. 1278).** From the British Museum website at tinyurl.com/lprzaaj.

61. **Figure 13: Egyptian ceramic dish (late 13th century).** In the Kunstgewerbemuseum [Textile art museum] Berlin; image from de Vries, line 54, crediting Joachim Gierlichs, "Drache, Phönix, Doppeladler" [Dragon, phoenix, double eagle] in *Fabelwesen in der islamischen Kunst* [Mythical creatures in Islamic art], Bilderhefte der Staatlichen Museen zu Berlin [Picturebook of the state museums of Berlin] (1993), vol. 75/76, p. 60, no. 81.

62. **Figure 14: Egyptian postherd.** From Leo A. Mayer, *Saracenic Heraldry* (Oxford, 1933), plate 3 no. 2.

63. **Figure 15: Egyptian postherd.** *Id.*, plate 3, no 3.

64. **Figure 16: Brocade from Palermo (before 1309).** From Soloviev (1935), line 49, 128, fig. 8.

65. **Figure 17: Sculpted roundel from Palermo Cathedral (12th century).** From Androudis (2013), line 46, 214, fig. 6.

66. **Figure 18: Gold tari coin from Messina mint, Sicily, issued in the name of Frederick II (c. 1202).** Image from the Sixbid coin auction website at tinyurl.com/orqmz8l.

67. **Figure 19: Textile fragment from the "Cloak of the Virgin" in Thiur, France (Islamic Spain, 12th century).** In the Musée des Tissus [Textile museum], Lyon, France. Image from de Vries, line 54.

68. **Figure 20: Silk fragment from the tomb of Saint Bernard of Calvó in the Cathedral of Vich, Spain, (Islamic Spain, 1071-1106).** In the Metropolitan Museum of Art, New York. Image from de Vries, line 54.

69. **Figure 21: Textile fragment (Islamic Spain, 12th century).** Line drawing by Fidèle-Gabriel in Gevaert. line 5, p. 46, fig. 69. A photograph can be seen in Gierlichs, line 61, p. 60, no. 81. The original is in the Kunstgewerbemuseum [Textile art museum], Berlin.

70. **Figure 22: Detail from the Shroud of St. Amadus (Islamic Spain, 11th century).** In the collection of the Abegg-Stiftung [Abegg Foundation], Riggisberg, Switzerland. Image from de Vries, line 54.

71. **Figure 23: Bas-relief from church of St. Martin, Gensac-La-Pollue, France (12th century).** Image from Androudis (2013), line 46, p. 220, fig. 14.

72. **Figure 24: Tiles from Abbey Church of Vivoin, France (13th century).** Drawing by Fidèle-Gabriel in Gevaert, line 5, p. 106, fig. 173.

73. **Figure 25: Detail from a fresco in Clermont Cathedral, France (12th century).** *Id.*, p. 44, fig. 67.

74. **Figure 26: Detail of a fresco in Church of Saint-Hilaire in Asnières-sur-Vègre, France (12th century).** Image from Androudis (2013), line 46, p, 220, fig. 16.

75. **Figure 27:** [reserved]

76. **Figure 28: Illuminated initial from French manuscript (c. 1150).** Image from *id.*, fig. 15. Originally from a manuscript of *Glosae in Psalmos de Gilbertus Porretanus* [Commentary on the Psalms by Gilbert of Poitiers], ms. 0020, p. 196v, in the Bibliothèque Municipale [Municipal library], Vendôme, France.

77. **Figure 29: Line drawing of an eagle detail on the "Shroud of St. Germanus" (Byzantine, 11th century).** From Geneviève Saint-Martin, *L'Aigle* [The eagle] (Puiseaux [France], 1996), 74. The original is in the museum of the Abbey of St.-Germain in Auxerre, France. Saint-Martin erroneously dates this fabric to the fifth century.

78. **Figure 30: Miniature of Sebastocrator Constantine Palaeologos and his wife Eirene (1310).** From the Lincoln Typikon at the Bodleian Library, Oxford. Image from Wikimedia Commons at tinyurl.com/n8cm5az.

79. **Figure 31: Locket of Princess Tamar (1294).** In the Museo Archeologico Nazionale [National archaeological museum] in Cividale dei Friuli, Italy. Image from Donald M. Nicol, *The Byzantine Lady* (Cambridge, 1996), plate 2.

80. **Figure 32: Relief in the Church of the Parigoritissa, Arta (c. 1295).** From Charalampos Chotzakoglou, "Die Palaiologen und das früheste Auftreten des byzantinischen Doppeladlers" [The Palaeologues and the first appearance of the Byzantine double eagle], *Byzantinoslavica* (Prague, 1996), 57:60, plate 10, fig. 11. Credited to A. K. Orlandos, *Parēgoritissa tēs Artēs* [Parigoritissa of Arta] (Athens, 1968), fig. 108.

81. **Figure 33: Marble slab from Metropolitan church of Mistra, 15th century.** Image from Wikimedia Commons at tinyurl.com/pz48anq.

82. **Figure 34: Earring of Maria Palaeologina, Queen of Serbia (early 14th century).** In the Archaeological Museum of Skopje, Macedonia. Image from Chotzakoglou, line 80, plate 11, figure 14. Credited to Biaga Alexova, "Gde je sahranjena Mari ja Paleologova?" [Where was Maria Palaeologina buried?], *Anali Zavoda* (Dubrovnik, 1956), 4-5:213-39.

83. **Figure 35: Four faces of a capital in the Basilica of St. Demetrios, Thessalonika (first half of the 14th century).** By Pascal Androudis, from his "Chapiteau de la crypte de la basilique de Saint-Démétrios à Thessalonique avec emblèmes de la famille des Paléologues" [Capital in the crypt of the basilica of St, Demetrios in Thessalonika with emblems of the Palaeologue family], Deltion of the Christian Archaeological Society of Greece (Athens, 2012), 51:131-140, p. 132, fig. 2.

84. **Figure 36: Byzantine double eagle with Palaeologue monogram.** Line drawing from Andrea Babuin, "Standards and Insignia of Byzantium," *Byzantion* (Brussels, 2001), 71(1):5-59, at 57, no. 86. Babuin, at 52, identifies this image "the device of emperor John VIII Palaeologos, Psalter XVI century?, Sinaiticus Gr. 2123, f. 133, Monastery of St. Catherine, Mount Sinai." For a color image, variously attributed to a church fresco, a prayer book of Demetrios Palaeologos, and (as noted) a post-Byzantine binding on the *Codex Sinaiticus*, see Wikimedia Commons at tinyurl.com/pqy9joa.

85. **Figure 37: Gattilusi inscription, Chorea, Samothrace (1433).** Photograph by Robert Ousterhout in his "Byzantium between East and West and the Origins of Heraldry," in Colum Hourihane, ed., *Byzantine Art: Recent Studies* [Arizona Studies in the Middle Ages and Renaissance] (Tempe [Arizona], 2009), 33:153-170161, fig. 7.

86. **Figure 38: Frecso of Manuel I of Trebizond, from Hagia Sophia of Trebizond (mid-13th century).** Image from Chotzakoglou, line 80, plate 9, figure 10, after a drawing by Prince Grigory Grigorievich Gagarin. Credited to David Talbot Rice, *The Church of Haghia Sophia at Trebizond* (Edinburgh 1968), fig. 79.

87. **Figure 39: Galley cabin of Emperor John VIII.** Line drawing by Noah Phillips, after the Filarete bronze door (1445), line 19.

88. **Figure 40: Printer's mark of Zacarias Calliergi (Venice, 1499).** Image from Wikimedia Commons at tinyurl.com/oxdf5px. For a view of the original *in situ*, see the digitization of the *Etymologicum Magnum* (p. 472) on the Anemi Digital Library of Modern Greek Studies website of the University of Crete at tinyurl.com/mqsbuba.

89. **Figure 41. Byzantine banner embroidery (c. 1366-70).** From Kathrin Colburn, "A Double-Headed Eagle Embroidery: Analysis and Conservation," *Metropolitan Museum Journal* (New York, 2006), 41:65-74, 72, fig. 7.

90. **Figure 42: Detail of head from Figure 41.** *Id.*, 67, fig. 3.

91. **Figure 43: Detail of foot from Figure 41.** *Id.*, 71, fig. 6.

92. **Figure 44: Brooch of Gisela of Swabia (10th century).** From Freerk Kaye Hamkens, *Alte Deutsche Reichsadler* [Old German national eagles] (Brussels, 1944), figure 1. For an explanation of the word *Reichsadler*, see note 83 on page 34 above.

93. **Figure 45: Silver penny of Leopold V of Austria (1197).** Untraceable Internet image of coin.

94. **Figure 46: Wall tile from Abbey Church of St. Emmeram, Regensburg (mid-12th century).** In the Germanisches Nationalmuseum [German national museum], Nuremberg. Image from Anna Pawlik, "Ornament und Eleganz" [Ornament and elegance], from the museum's publication *KulturGut* (Nuremberg, 2013), p. 2, fig. 2, on the museum's website at tinyurl.com/qaunjdh.

95. **Figure 47: Seal of Count Ludwig von Sarwarden (c. 1185).** From Friedrich Karl von Hohenlohe-Waldenburg [Prince Hohenlohe], *Sphragistische Aphorismen: 300 mittel-alterliche Siegel Systematisch Classificiert und erläutert* [Sphragistic aphorisms: 300 medieval seals systematically classified and explained] (Heilbronn, 1882), 111, on Project Gutenberg at tinyurl.com/po9f88y; image reprinted in Gustav Seyler, *Die Siegel* [Seals] (Leipzig, 1894), 89, fig. 34.

96. **Figure 48: Seal of Poppo, Count of Henneberg (c. 1212).** From Seyler, line 95, 273, fig. 327.

97. **Figure 49: Seal of Heinrich von Kirkel (1240).** *Id.*, 356, fig. 377.

98. **Figure 50: Supposed arms of Emperor Frederick II. c. 1258.** From Matthew Paris, *Historia Anglorum*, in the British Library, III:149r. The whole book can be seen, and images enlarged and captured, on the British Library's website at tinyurl.com/og97g93.

99. **Figure 51: *Augustalis* of Frederick II.** From Wikimedia Commons at tinyurl.com/ldfyhpx; attributed to Classical Numismatic Group, Inc., www.cngcoins.com.

100. **Figure 52: Coin of Otto IV (reigned 1198-1218).** Image from Cappe, line 10, part I, plate 22, no. 368, illustrating 1:154, no. 692.

101. **Figure 53: Seal of infant Wenceslaus IV, King of Bohemia (1363).** From Otto Posse, *Die Siegel der Deutschen Kaiser und Könige: von 751 bis 1806* [The seals of the German emperors and kings from 751 to 1806] (Dresden, 1913), vol. 2, plate 7, no. 3. The text accompanying this image is found in vol. 5, p. 43. The entire five-volume work (Dresden, 1909-13) is available on Wikimedia Commons at tinyurl.com/mcmsv6r, digitized for the (German) de.Wikisource by Saarländische Universitäts- und Landesbibliothek [State university and library of the Saar], Saarbrücken. Image redrawn by Charles Waltmire from the muddy 100-year-old photograph in Posse.

102. **Figure 54: Seal of Emperor Sigismund.** From Posse, line 101, vol. 2, plate 17, no. 2. The text accompanying this image is found in vol. 5, p. 43.

103. **Figure 55: Seal of City of Friedberg (1260).** Modern facsimile by Historic Waxcraft, Rochester, New York. See www.historicseals.net.

104. **Figure 56: Seal of City of Friedberg (1344).** *Ibid.*

105. **Figure 57: Seal of City of Kaiserswerd.** From Seyler, line 95, 308, fig. 303.

106. **Figure 58: City banner of Cologne (c. 1500).** In the Kölnisches Stadtmuseum [City museum of Cologne]; image from the Geman Bildindex website at tinyurl.com/qduu4xr.

107. **Figure 59: Seal of the Jewish community in Augsburg (1298).** From P. Jaffé, "Ein Siegel der Juden zu Augsburg vom Jahre 1298" [A seal of the Jews of Augsburg from 1298], in *Literaturblatt des Orients: Berichte, Studien und Kritiken für jüdische Geschichte und Literatur* [Literary journal of the East: Reports, studies and reviews on Jewish history and

literature] (Leipzig, 1842), vol. 5, no. 73. Image reprinted, with commentary, in Sabine Ullmann, "Judentum in Schwaben (bis 1800)" [Jewry in Swabia to 1800], on the website of the Historisches Lexikon Bayerns [Historical dictionary of Bavaria] at tinyurl.com/ncdassa.

108.   **Figure 60: Thalers of imperial cities during the reign of Charles V.** Detail from John Porteous, *Coins in History* (New York, 1969), 160, fig. 179.

109.   **Figure 61: Imperial banner (1545).** Woodcut by Jacob Kallenberg, from Jacob Köbel, *Wapen des Heyligen Römischen Reichs Teutscher Nation* [Arms of the Holy Roman Empire of the German nation] (Frankfurt, 1545). Image from Wikimedia Commons at tinyurl.com/mme7b5r; original digitized on the website of the Bayerischen Staatsbibliothek [Bavarian state library] at tinyurl.com/l3me49y.

110.   **Figure 62: Lübeck boundary marker (contemporary).** Photograph by Jan Tappenbeck, from Wikimedia Commons at tinyurl.com/kkeydhv.

111.   **Figure 63: Imperial crown (so-called Crown of Charlemagne).** Line drawing by Tiete van der Laars in *Wapens, Vlaggen en Zegels van Nederland* [Arms, flags and seals of the Netherlands] (Amsterdam, 1913), 10, fig. 45.

112.   **Figure 64: Crown of Emperor Frederick III (1493).** From his tomb sculpture. Line drawing by Emil Doepler the Younger (1855-1921), in Friedrich Warnecke, *Heraldisches Handbuch* [Heraldic handbook], a pattern book (Görlitz, 1880; modern reprint Limburg, 1971), plate 21.

113.   **Figure 65: Emperor Sigismund at the Council of Constance.** Woodcut from Ulrich von Richenthal, *Chronik des Constanzer Konzils* [Chronicle of the Council of Constance] (Augsburg, 1483). The 1483 edition is the first printed version of Richenthal's 1480 manuscript. This image (from Hamkens, line 92, plate 4) does not appear in the modern facsimile by Richard Michael Buck, ed., *Ulrich von Richenthal: Chronik des Constanzer Conzils* (Leipzig, 1936), or in the digitalized facsimile on the Heidelberg University website at tinyurl.com/lyftvy8.

114.   **Figure 66: Silver coin of Margaret of Constantinople (Flemish, 1244).** From the December 27, 2013 posting "Double-Headed Eagle in the West Part 3" on the Russian Philologist website at tinyurl.com/n2kkd7l.

115.   **Figure 67: Triple eagle page from *Grünenberg's Armorial* (1483).** This image, digitized from the original in the Bayerische Staatsbibliothek [Bavarian state library], comes from the website of the Münchener DigitalizierungZentrum [Munich digitalizing center]. The frame shown is 00009. The whole book can be seen, and images enlarged and captured, on their website at tinyurl.com/mq7b835. See also frame 00007 for the triple eagle shield alone.

116.   **Figure 68: Gold coin of Charles V.** Internet image of coin.

117.   **Figure 69: Licensing page.** Giovanni Crisostomo Zanchi, *Ad Carolum V Panegyricus* [Panegyric to Charles V] (Rome, 1536?). The image is from the University of Pennsylvania Rare Books Library in Philadelphia, posted to the Internet through the Penn Provenance Project launched jointly with Flickr; see tinyurl.com/q5drzyg. This image can be found on Flickriver at tinyurl.com/mju8qqh.

118.   **Figure 70: Dedication page.** Francisco López de Xerez, *Conquista del Peru & Provincia del Cuzco de le Indie Occidentali* [Conquest of Peru and the province of Cuzco in the West Indies] (Venice, 1535), vol. 1. Source of image as for line 117.

119.   **Figure 71: Arms from imperial edict.** Published by Servaeus Sassenus (Louvain, 1550). Source of image as for line 117.

120.   **Figure 72: Woodcut by Heinrich Vogtherr the Elder (c. 1547-48).** Image from Wikimedia Commons at tinyurl.com/mz725p5. Modern publication in Schrade, line 8, fig. 23.

121.   **Figure 73: City gate of Toledo, Spain.** Line drawing by Ignacio Vicente Cascante, from his *Heráldica General*, line 14, 480, fig. 301.

122.   **Figure 74: Arms of Academia Boyacense de Historia. Tunja, Colombia.** From Javier Ocampo López, "Falleció Enrique Medina Flórez, Ilustre Escritor y Poeta Tunjano" [Illustrious writer and poet of Tunja], posted on April 10, 2013 to the Vemos y Escuchamos [We see and hear] blog page at tinyurl.com/lybn7wl.

123.   **Figure 75: Double eagle and snake.** From the mission church (Mision Jalpan) in Jalpan de Serra, Querétaro, Mexico, from the "Aztec Eagle" post on the Colonial Mexico blogspot (August 13, 2012) at tinyurl.com/kosdy84.

124.   **Figure 76: Mystical Arms of Spain.** From Juan de Caramuel y Lobkowitz, *Declaración Mystica de las Arms de España* (Brussels, 1636). Image from Immaculada Rodriguez and Victor Minguez, "Symbolical Explanation of the Spanish Coats of Arms According to Juan de Caramuel (1636)," *Emblematica* (New York, 2008), 16:223-251, 238.

125.   **Figure 77: Flag of the Austrian Netherlands.** From Wikimedia Commons, at tinyurl.com/kl6rv2y.

126.   **Figure 78: Seal of Engelbert Ludick van Dijck (1318).** From A. H. Hoeben, *Brabantse Heraldiek in Historisch Perspectief* [Heraldry of Brabant in historic perspective] (The Hague, 1991), 54, fig. 5.26.

127.   **Figure 79: Arms of the Margraves of Antwerp.** Woodcut from Michiel Hillen van Hoochstraaten, *Evangelien ende epistelen mette sermonen van de gheleelen iare …* [Gospels and epistles with sermons for the whole year …] (Antwerp, 1500). In the Museum Plantijn Moretus, Antwerp; illustrated in Hubert de Vries, *Wapens van de Nederlanden* [Arms of the Netherlands] (Amsterdam, 1995), 74.

128.   **Figure 80: Arms of Johan Lodewijk van Elderen, Prince-Bishop of Liège.** Photograph by H. P. de Vries, from the manuscript *Cartes Genéalogiques des Gentils-hommes* [Pedigrees of gentlemen] (1691), reproduced in Hubert de Vries, line 127, 117. The original is in the Archives d'État de Liège [State archives of Liège].

129.   **Figure 81. Modern city flag of Arnhem.** From Wikimedia Commons at tinyurl.com/ktnqv6l.

130.   **Figure 82: Small arms of Austrian Empire (1900).** By Hugo Gerard Ströhl (1900), line 2, plate 5.

131.   **Figure 83: Elaborated version of Austrian Empire genealogical arms (1880).** By Emil Doepler the Younger, from Warnecke, line 112, plate 27.

132. **Figure 84: "Full" arms of Austria.** By Agi Lindegren, from Wrangel, line 6, 1:21.

133. **Figure 85: Coronation medal of Ferdinand I (1558).** Image from the AC Search numismatic website at tinyurl.com/kvq3s2s.

134. **Figure 86: Great seal of Leopold I for Transylvania (1696).** From Posse, line 101, vol. 3, plate 68, no. 4.

135. **Figure 87: Eagle of the Hoch- und Deutschmeister.** Photograph posted to Pinterest by Judith Milledge, at tinyurl.com/kgg8eu4.

136. **Figure 88: Transylvanian gold ducat of Maria Theresa (1775).** Image from the Coinarchives website at tinyurl.com/kwja3ox (now hidden behind a paywall).

137. **Figure 89: Imperial great arms, 1915 pattern.** Line drawing by Hugo Gerard Ströhl; image from Franz Gall, *Österreichische Wappenkunde* [Austrian heraldry] (Vienna, 1966), 100.

138. **Figure 90: Maria Theresa thaler.** Internet image of coin. This is the reverse of the coin in line 27; see the text figure on page 51.

139. **Figure 91: Colour of an imperial cuirassier regiment.** From Robert Hall and Giancarlo Boeri, *Uniforms and Flags of the Imperial Austrian Army 1683-1720*, (n.p., 2008) (CD), plate CR09.

140. **Figure 92: Colour of a Hungarian heiduck regiment.** *Id.*, plate HR12, citing Jean Belaubre, *Les Triomphes des Louis le Grand* [The triumphs of Louis the great] (Paris, 1970).

141. **Figure 93. Colour of imperial Baden-Durlach infantry regiment.** From the German Flaggen-Versand24 website at tinyurl.com/p8kvwzc.

142. **Figure 94: Regimental flag of Austrian Walloon regiment, late 18th century.** By Guido Rosignoli, from Terence Wise, *Military Flags of the World 1618-1900* (New York, 1978), plate 39, no. 232. Walloons are French-speaking Catholics from the Netherlands.

143. **Figure 95: Schützkompanie Tramin colour (1779 pattern).** From the company's Austrian website at tinyurl.com/myx7n25.

144. **Figure 96: Austrian infantry colour of Maria Theresa (1754).** Image by Zdirad J. K. Čech, from Eva Gregorovičová and Pavel Sedláček, *Česka Panovická a Státní Symbolika* [Czech sovereign's and state's symbols] (Prague, 2002), 46, fig. 41.

145. **Figure 97: Austrian naval ensign (c. 1713).** Image by Željko Heimer, from the Flags of the World website at tinyurl.com/lw99rgq.

146. **Figure 98: German Confederation war flag.** Image by Jaume Ollé, from *id.* at tinyurl.com/kuxejpw.

147. **Figure 99: Small arms of Schwarzburg-Rudolstadt.** By Agi Lindegren, from Wrangel, line 6, 2:772.

148. **Figure 100: Austrian army belt buckle.** Image from the website of the Berlin-Military Thrift Shop at tinyurl.com/l652szs.

149. **Figure 101: Badge of the Austrian Order of the Iron Crown.** From Maximilian Gritzner, *Handbuch der Ritter- und Verdienstorden* [Handbook of knightly and service orders] (Leipzig 1893; modern reprint Graz, 1962), 278, fig. 339.

150. **Figure 102: Arms of (Austrian) Kingdom of Lombardy-Venetia.** Image from Wikimedia Commons at tinyurl.com/lwxpqco.

151. **Figure 103: Austro-Hungarian imperial standard (1894 pattern).** Image by Željko Heimer, from the Flags of the World website at tinyurl.com/khjf4f2.

152. **Figure 104: Title page of sheet music for Josef Franz Wagner, *Unter dem Doppeladler Marsch* (detail).** Published in Vienna in 1893 (Opus 159) [Under the double eagle march]. Image from Wikimedia Commons at tinyurl.com/ku7btud. I have not been able to discover the name of the artist.

153. **Figure 105: *Militärmark* of the Austrian 11th Dragoons.** Artist unknown; from Lotte Maier, *Militärmarken* [Military labels] (Dortmund, 1981), 97, fig. 2.

154. **Figure 106: Art deco design by Koloman Moser.** Image from Gall, line 137, 102.

155. **Figure 107: Emblem of the imperial Austrian Red Cross Society.** Image from Austrian Wikipedia at tinyurl.com/mhglder.

156. **Figure 108: Officials' rank flag of the Austrian Federal State (1936).** Image by Željko Heimer, from the Flags of the World website page for this regime at tinyurl.com/m7agpfd, citing *Militaria Austriaca: Ausbildungsvorschrift für die Pioniertruppe* [Training provisions for engineering troops] (Part 12, 1936).

157. **Figure 109: Emblem of Vienna (1938-45).** Image from Peter Diem, "Die Symbole Wiens" [Symbols of Vienna], on the Austria Forum website at tinyurl.com/lx27uma. With Dr. Diem's help I have traced this image to the cover of *Wiener Brevier* [Vienna breviary] (Vienna, 1943), vol. 79, no. 2, a magazine for soldiers published by the German Army High Command [*Oberkommando der Wehrmacht*]. Austria had by that time merged into Germany. The creator of this image remains unknown.

158. **Figure 110: Arms of Fiume.** By Hugo Gerard Ströhl (1900), line 2, plate 11.

159. **Figure 111: Armorial coin of Pope Alexander VIII (Ottoboni) (1589).** Image from the Rhinocoins numismatic website at tinyurl.com/kwn5egu.

160. **Figure 112: Arms of Garganelli.** From the Garganelli page of the website "I Nostri Avi" [Our ancestors], at tinyurl.com/n6m4vtp, where the image is said to have come from an Italian armorial in the Bayerische Staatsbibliothek [Bavarian state library].

161. **Figure 113: Arms of Seregi di Cortesia.** From Sovereign Military Order of [St. John of] Jerusalem and Malta, *Elenco Storico della Nobilità Italiana* [Historical directory of the Italian nobility] (Rome, 1960), 483.

162. **Figure 114: Arms of Filangeri.** From the Royal Filangeri genealogy site at tinyurl.com/n3xgyu3.

163. **Figure 115: Arms of Commune of Velletri.** Image by Massimo Ghirardi. From Italian Wikipedia at tinyurl.com/ook8mbt, crediting Araldica Civica (www.araldicacivica.it).

183. **Figure 135: Helmet of the Russian Life Guards Regiment.** From the website of the Hermitage Museum, St. Petersburg, at tinyurl.com/lz7wy7c. According to the museum label, this is not actually a real helmet, but a silver goblet made in the shape of one, presumably for the regimental mess.

184. **Figure 136: Arms of Chudovo.** From P. P. von-Vinkler, *Gerbi Gorodovi, Gobernii, Oblasteye i Rosalovi Rossiyeskoye Imperiye* ... [Arms of cities, governates, districts and outposts of the Russian Empire] (St. Petersburg, 1899; modern reprint Moscow, n.d.), 213.

185. **Figure 137: Colour-staff finial from a Russian Guards Regiment.** Detail from Vladimir Zvegintsov, *Znamena i Shtandarti Russkoye Armee XVI vek – 1914 i Morskiye Flagi* [Flags and standards of the Russian army, 16th century – 1914, and naval flags] (Moscow, 2008), 255.

186. **Figure 138: Russian military guidon (17th century).** *Id.*, 152, fig. 50.

187. **Figure 139: Colour of the Ryazan Carabineer Regiment (1763).** From an eBay Internet auction listing.

188. **Figure 140: Colonel's colour, Guards Artillery Train and Bombardier Company.** From Max Barry, "The Imperial Russian Army in Detail," on his NationStates website at tinyurl.com/oeq9ccy.

189. **Figure 141: Russian line infantry regimental colour (1803 standard pattern).** By Guido Rosignoli, from Terence Wise, *Flags of the Napoleonic Wars* (London, 1978), 2:32.

190. **Figure 142. Flag of an imperial Russian minister plenipotentiary.** From *Flags of Maritime Nations*, line 3, 56.

191. **Figure 143: Russian imperial standard for use afloat (1858 pattern).** *Id.*, 52.

192. **Figure 144: Seal of the Russian Provisional Government (1917).** From Pauli Kruhse, "The Collection of Decrees of the Grand Duchy of Finland, No. 20," on his History of Finland website at tinyurl.com/p6v83fa.

193. **Figure 145: Russian state standard (19th century).** From Vilinbakov, line 180, 124.

194. **Figure 146: Arms of Russian Federation (1993 pattern).** From Wikimedia Commons at tinyurl.com/l5795e5.

195. **Figure 147: Ruble coin (2014).** Untraceable Internet image.

196. **Figure 148: Russian Presidential standard (1994 pattern).** From Vilinbakov, line 180, 159.

197. **Figure 149: Flag of "Donetsk People's Republic" (2014).** Vector image by Peter Orensky, from a news photograph. Reproduced by courtesy of the artist.

198. **Figure 150: Seal of Skanderbeg.** From Brahaj, line 36, 91, fig. 2.

199. **Figure 151: Supposed arms of Skanderbeg.** From "Albania's Double-Headed Eagle Symbol: Scanderbeg's Personal Emblem and Standard" on the Frosina website at tinyurl.com/mdygj6l.

200. **Figure 152: Flag of the Principality of Albania (1914).** By Jaume Ollé, from the Flags of the World website at tinyurl.com/krmwhvv.

201. **Figure 153: Historical design by Charles F. B. Morse.** From Brahaj, line 36, 146. This image appeared in the first issue of the Albanian nationalist newspaper *Trumbéta é Krujes* [Trumpets of Krujë], published in St. Louis [Missouri] on March 20, 1911. The two panels were originally side by side, separated by information about the newspaper. For the original format, and slightly more about the image, see the February 22, 2014 posting on the Pashtriku website at <u>tinyurl.com/lnn2nmq</u> (in Albanian). Krujë was one of the original sites of Skanderbeg's resistance to the Turks.

202. **Figure 154: Standard of Prince Vili I (Wilhelm of Wied).** Source of image as for line 200.

203. **Figure 155: Albanian national flag (1992 pattern).** Image from Wikimedia Commons at <u>tinyurl.com/yk4rhz2</u>.

204. **Figure 156: Albanian national arms (1992 pattern).** Image from Wikimedia Commons at <u>tinyurl.com/l6cp6u6</u>.

205. **Figure 157: Albanian revenue stamp (1920).** Image from the eBay auction website. The design is type D5 in Scott's Standard Postage Stamp Catalogue.

206. **Figure 158: Albanian gold coin (1927).** Internet image of coin.

207. **Figure 159: Flag image for Serbia from the map of Angelino Dulcert (1339).** From Alexander Soloviev, *Istoria Srpskog Grba* [History of the Serbian arms] (Belgrade, 1958; modern reprint 2000), 366. An expandable facsimile of the map appears on Wikimedia Commons at <u>tinyurl.com/mpu79xn</u>. Soloviev's book is a valuable treasury of Serbian double eagles and official symbolism, but it is in Serbian.

208. **Figure 160: Ring of Queen Teodora (mid-14th century).** From Soloviev (1958), line 207, plate 24, no. 3.

209. **Figure 161: Fresco of Prince Miroslav in Byzantine-style robe, Bijelo Polje, Montenegro.** Drawing by A. Deroko, from *id.*, plate 23, no. 1.

210. **Figure 162: Metal roundel from a chandelier in the Markov monastery, Skopje (c. 1366).** In the State Museum of Serbia, Belgrade. Image from Soloviev (1958), line 207, plate 23, no. 6.

211. **Figure 163: Coin of Bulgarian Emperor Michael Shishman (1327).** Image from Nikola Moushmov, *Ancient Coins of the Balkan Peninsula and the Coins of the Bulgarian Monarchs* (Sofia, 1912), plate 67 no. 5. The work appears in English translation on the Wildwinds coin website at <u>www.wildwinds.com/moushmov</u>. Redrawn by Charles Waltmire.

212. **Figure 164: Arms of Nemanjić from the Korenić-Neorić Armorial (1595).** From the facsimile of the armorial on a Japanese blog at <u>tinyurl.com/m6hlzog</u>.

213. **Figure 165: Arms of Stefan Lazarević (1483).** From Ulrich von Richenthal's *Chronik des Constanzer Konzils*, 108v. See line 113. This image is from Soloviev (1935), line 49, 142, fig. 15.

214. **Figure 166:** [reserved]

215. **Figure 167. Arms of Serbia from the *Stematografija* (1741).** From Žefarović, line 45, 30.

216.   **Figure 168: Seal of Karageorge.** Detail, from the Russian Vetarsabalkana website at tinyurl.com/mcqx37s.

217.   **Figure 169: Serbian royal arms (1899).** By Agi Lindegren, from Wrangel, line 6, 2:784.

218.   **Figure 170: Serbian state flag (1882 pattern).** Image by Mario Febretto, from the Flags of the World website at tinyurl.com/krean5h.

219.   **Figure 171: Arms of Obrenović Dynasty.** Image from Wikimedia Commons at tinyurl.com/mmkbfxg.

220.   **Figure 172: Arms of King Stephan Lazarević as a Knight of the Dragon.** From Dushan Mrćenović, *Rodoslovne Tabletse i Grbovi Srpskich Dinastiya i Vlastele* [Genealogical tables and arms of Serbian dynasties and nobility] (Belgrade, 1987), 72. Although I have often seen this image reproduced, for example in Soloviev (1958), line 207, plate 4 no. 1, I have not been able to trace it to an early source.

221.   **Figure 173: Yugoslav royal arms (c. 1922).** Image by Željko Heimer, from the Flags of the World website at tinyurl.com/lbofvk8.

222.   **Figure 174: Arms of Yugoslav Kingdom and Yugoslav royal arms (c. 1933).** Title page of Emilij Laszowski and Rudolf Horvat, *Grbovi Jugoslavije* [Coats of Arms of Yugoslavia] (Zagreb, c. 1931-34), a Kava [Coffee] Hag civic armorial album. Artist unknown, but perhaps Laszowski. The royal arms are above the national arms. Thanks to Ralf Hartemink for help with this source. For more on the Café Hag civic heraldry albums, see his Heraldry of the World website at tinyurl.com/m2rqjes.

223.   **Figure 175: Yugoslav royal standard (1937 pattern).** Image from Wikimedia Commons at tinyurl.com/n8kzrm4.

224.   **Figure 176: Serbian Order of the White Eagle.** From Juan Carlos Mantel, *Orders/Ordines* (Buenos Aires, 1998), vol. 1, fig. SER 160.

225.   **Figure 177: Arms of State Union of Serbia and Montenegro (2006).** Image from Wikimedia Commons at tinyurl.com/ldo6v5u.

226.   **Figure 178: Serbian national flag (2009 pattern).** Image by Željko Heimer, from the Flags of the World website at tinyurl.com/lh45d9t.

227.   **Figure 179: Serbian presidential standard (2009 pattern).** Image from Wikimedia Commons at tinyurl.com/k3lzm7v.

228.   **Figure 180: Colour of the Serbian Air Force (reverse) (2010).** Image by Ivan Sarajčić, from the Flags of the World website at tinyurl.com/lcps43d, crediting the Serbian Armed Forces website.

229.   **Figure 181. City flag of Leskovac, Serbia.** Image from Wikimedia Commons at tinyurl.com/m9rjfdy.

230.   **Figure 182: *Graffito* from a Vienna park (circa 1992).** From the Graffitieuropa website at tinyurl.com/kjdtmdo, citing Graffiti-News no. 15 (May 19, 2002).

231.   **Figure 183: Heading page of the *Oktoih Prvoglasnik*.** Published in Cetinje, 1494. Reproduced from the facsimile published by the Central National Montenegrin Library

(Cetinje, 1987); image from the Montenegrin "Digital Library of Montenegrin Culture" website at tinyurl.com/jwfmc9f.

232.   **Figure 184: Montenegrin Military Bravery Medal (1841).** From the Liveauctioneers Internet auction website at tinyurl.com/k7ydfyj.

233.   **Figure 185: Arms of Montenegro (1899).** By Agi Lindegren, from Wrangel, line 6, 2:482.

234.   **Figure 186: Montenegrin gold 100-perper coin (1910).** Image from German Wikimedia at tinyurl.com/k7fujbk.

235.   **Figure 187: Nineteenth century Montenegrin flag.** Image from Dragana Samarjich, *Vojne Zastave Srba do 1918* [Serbian military flags to 1918] (Belgrade, 1983), fig. 90.

236.   **Figure 188: Standard of Prince Danilo I (1852).** Image by Mario Febretto, from the Flags of the World website at tinyurl.com/n9xkzaz, citing Aldo Ziggioto, "Armi e Bandiere del Montenegro: Molte Ombre e Poche Luci" [Arms and flags of Montenegro: Many shadows and a few lights], *Archivum Heraldicum* [Heraldic archive] (Lausanne, 1989 no. 2).

237.   **Figure 189: Arms of Montenegro (1993).** Image from Wikimedia Commons at tinyurl.com/lub6n4r.

238.   **Figure 190: Montenegrin national flag (2004 pattern).** Image from Wikimedia Commons at tinyurl.com/23an58b.

239.   **Figure 191: Seal of Guilliame de l'Aigle (1278).** From the Histoire de L'Ordre du Temple [History of the Templar Order] page on the website of the National Archives of France, S. 4995, n° 149 (DA 9868), see tinyurl.com/lv3zxr8. Redrawn by Charles Waltmire.

240.   **Figure 192: Arms of Perth, Scotland.** From Arthur C. Fox-Davies, *The Book of Public Arms*, (Edinburgh, 1915 edition), 601. Despite the monogram signature in this drawing, I have been unable to identify the artist.

241.   **Figure 193: Danish local seal.** Seal of Års Herred, Holbæk County, Denmark, by Johan Kristian Kongstad, in Thorkild Gravlund, *Herredsbogen* [Shire book] (Copenhagen, 1926-30). Image from Danish Wikimedia at tinyurl.com/lxebstl.

242.   **Figure 194: Copper shilling of Mihnea III (Michael Radu), Prince of Wallachia (1658).** From the Coinarchives website at tinyurl.com/mgnsscy.

243.   **Figure 195: Flag of the Russian-American Company.** Image from Wikimedia Commons at tinyurl.com/m75z2gk, taken from Собрание Штандартов, Флагов и Вымпелов, употребляемых в Российской империи [The standard of the Assembly, flags and pennants, used in the Russian Empire] (St. Petersburg, 1835).

244.   **Figure 196: Emblem of 33° Mason, Scottish Rite.** From the Freemason Collection website at tinyurl.com/lmgzrbp.

245.   **Figure 197: Mysore revenue stamp (detail).** Author's collection. The stamp is Type 65 in Adolph Koeppel and Raymond D. Manners, *The Court Fee and Revenue Stamps of the Princely States of India* (Mineola [New York], 1989), 1:243.

246. **Figure 198: Golden jeweled cloak fitting (Hungarian, 13th century).** In the Hungarian National Museum, Budapest. Image from Zsuzsa Lovag, "Tasselpaar mit Doppeladler," on the University of Klagenfurt website at tinyurl.com/nb83vn7.

247. **Figure 199: French floor tiles (13th century).** Drawing by Fidèle-Gabriel in Gevaert, line 5, 46, fig. 70.

248. **Figure 200: Alchemical image from the *Buch der Heiligen Dreifaltigkeit* [Book of the Holy Trinity] (early 15th century).** Page 24 of the manuscript in the Bayerische Staatsbibliothek [Bavarian state library] in Munich (CGM.598). The image is from the article "The Imagery in the *Buch der heiligen Dreifaltigkeit*," on the Alchemy Website at tinyurl.com/pw64vkk.

249. **Figure 201: Reliquary from Zara (15th century).** Drawing by Herbert Cole, from his *Heraldry and Floral Forms Used in Decoration* (New York, 1922), 58.

250. **Figure 202: Gothic cloister window from Basilica of Our Lady, Maastricht, Netherlands (completed 1559).** Image on Wikimedia Commons at tinyurl.com/nxfplth.

251. **Figure 203: *Quaternionhumpen* (1615).** In the Deutsches Historisches Museum [German historical museum] in Berlin. Photograph by Michail Jungierek, from German Wikimedia at tinyurl.com/lrglgk9.

252. **Figure 204: German glass bottle (1615).** From the Dr. Fischer Kunstauktionen [Art auctions] website at tinyurl.com/k4fhr87, citing Karlheinz Joos, "Vierkantflasche mit Doppeladler" [Square bottle with double eagle] in *Der Glasfreund: Zeitschrift für Glassammler* [The glass friend: a glass collectors' journal] (Neustrelitz, May 2009), no. 31, p. 28.

253. **Figure 205: Italian armor.** Untraceable Internet image.

254. **Figure 206: Wallenstein's carved bureau (detail).** From "Das Doktorsgärtlein [the doctor's little garden] in Altdorf bei Nürnberg," on the Netzhautgruppe-Mittelfranken website at tinyurl.com/l6tzum4.

255. **Figure 207: Weathervane from Cologne.** From J. Kuiper, *De Heraldiek in Bouwkunst en Aanverwante Vakken* [Heraldry in architecture and related fields] (Amsterdam, 1910), 138.

256. **Figure 208: Hyacinth "La Bella."** In the *Schatzkammer* [Treasury] of the Hofburg [Imperial palace] in Vienna. Image from Pinterest at tinyurl.com/kkx6fdo.

257. **Figure 209: Tyrolean hanging cabinet (18th century).** In the Österreichisches Museum für Volkskunde [Austrian folk art museum], Vienna. Photograph by Andreas Praefke, from Wikimedia Commons at tinyurl.com/karalwz.

258. **Figure 210: Russian painted wood panel (c. 1740).** From Russian Bibliotekar website at tinyurl.com/lsp8czz.

259. **Figure 211: Italian faïence pitcher (c. 1770) (detail).** From an Internet auction website, now untraceable.

260. **Figure 212: Spanish colonial book stand.** Image from 1stDibs antiques website at tinyurl.com/msaxf3k.

261.   **Figure 213: Metal grille from Heart of Jesus chapel, church of Cayara, near Potosí, Bolivia.** Image from an unnamed German travel blog (posted November 20, 2013) at tinyurl.com/mk6dwnm.

262.   **Figure 214: Window from Zazarino Palace, Moscow (late 18th century).** From German GEO Reisecommunity website (posted May 14, 2010) at tinyurl.com/n2yhoeh.

263.   **Figure 215: German iron stove plate (1787).** From the website of the German auction house of Michael Zeller, at tinyurl.com/l39ewe5.

264.   **Figure 216: Roof of St. Stephen's Cathedral, Vienna (1831).** Photograph by Günni Gauner, posted October 15, 2007 on her blog page at tinyurl.com/lssc8lm.

265.   **Figure 217: Silver belt clasp from Troyan in Bulgaria (late 19th century).** In the British Museum; image from their website at tinyurl.com/nu84k5o.

266.   **Figure 218: Russian lace.** From Alan Summerly Cole, "Lace," in *Encyclopaedia Britannica* (New York, 1911), 16:45, figure 46.

267.   **Figure 219: Russian watch case.** From Krivchov, line 177, p. 178.

268.   **Figure 220: Brass hand mirror (Bulgarian? c.1900?).** From the eBay Internet auction website.

269.   **Figure 221: Russian enameled egg (1910).** Attributed to the Moscow workshop of Gregory Mikhailovich Zbitniev. Exhibited at the Frankfurter Ikonen-Museum [Frankfurt icon museum]; image from "Luxus der Zarenzeit" [Luxury in the time of the tsars], posted March 30, 2009, on the German Op-Online website at tinyurl.com/mhk8ym8.

270.   **Figure 222: Hood ornament, Russo-Balt fire engine (1912).** In the Rīgas Motormuzejs [Riga motor museum], Riga, Latvia; image from Wikimedia Commons at tinyurl.com/kxz3l6u.

271.   **Figure 223: Russian war loan poster (1916) (detail).** From N. I. Babuina and A. S. Kulemin, *Russkiye Plakat Pervoyi Mirovoyi Voeni* [Russian posters of World War I] (Moscow, 1992), 69.

272.   **Figure 224: Austrian war loan poster (1917).** By Heinrich Leffler, in the Library of Congress. Image from the "Lookandlearn History Picture Library" website at tinyurl.com/kfcwpj7.

273.   **Figure 225: Brass candlestick with arms of Lübeck (c. 1920).** From the eBay auction website.

274.   **Figure 226: Dust jacket from 1963 German edition of Jean Cocteau's *L'Aigle à Deux Têtes*.** Untraceable Internet image.

275.   **Figure 227: Stencil graffito (Austrian, 2005).** Image from Wikimedia Commons at tinyurl.com/mfh7oyc.

276. **Figure 228: *Doppeladler*, by Hans Crepaz.** Reproduced with the kind permission of the Galerie Unterlechner in Schwaz, Austria [www.galerieunterlechner.at].

277. **Figure 229: Greek AEK football emblem T-shirt (contemporary).** From the "T-Shirts I Want" website at tinyurl.com/kj7v7qk.

278. **Figure 230: Austrian cooking patch (contemporary).** From the German eBay auction website.

COLOPHON

This book was composed on a Microsoft Word word processing system,
with the aid of a Hewlett-Packard Scanjet 3500C image scanner.
It was printed with Flint soy-based inks
on 60-pound offset paper (12 point C2S paper for the covers)
by Specialty Graphics, Inc., of San Leandro, California,
on a Harris M-700 web press (text)
and a Komori Lithrone 40 sheet-fed press (covers),
using PDF Workflow and Kodak EVO digital publishing programs.
The type font is Times Roman, 13 point for the main body text,
12 point for picture sources, and 11 point for footnotes and captions.
The first printing, in November 2014, was 1600 copies.

ABOUT THE AUTHOR

David F. Phillips is a heraldic scholar in San Francisco. Trained as a lawyer and a librarian, he has been studying in this field for more than 60 years, and is the general editor of this series. He is the author of *Emblems of the Indian States* (2011); some of his other heraldic writing may be seen on his website at www.radbash.com/heraldry. He can be reached either through his website or at dfp18@columbia.edu.